VIOLENCE

Unless Recalled Earlier

Other titles in the
Forensic Psychotherapy Monograph Series

Forensic Psychotherapy and Psychopathology: Winnicottian Perspectives, edited by Brett Kahr

Life within Hidden Worlds: Psychotherapy in Prisons, edited by Jessica Williams Saunders

VIOLENCE

A Public Health Menace
and a Public Health Approach

Edited by

Sandra L. Bloom

Forensic Psychotherapy Monograph Series

Series Editor   Honorary Consultant
Brett Kahr   *Estela Welldon*

London & New York
KARNAC BOOKS

First published in 2001 by
H. Karnac (Books) Ltd.
6 Pembroke Buildings, Scrubs Lane, London NW10 6RE
A subsidiary of Other Press LLC, New York

British Library Cataloguing in Publication Data
A C.I.P. for this book is available from the British Library

  ISBN 1 85575 192 5

10 9 8 7 6 5 4 3 2 1

Edited, designed, and produced by Communication Crafts
Printed in Great Britain by Polestar Wheatons Ltd, Exeter

www.karnacbooks.com

CONTENTS

SERIES FOREWORD

Brett Kahr

School of Psychotherapy and Counselling,
Regent's College, London

Throughout most of human history, our ancestors have done rather poorly when dealing with acts of violence. To cite but one of many shocking examples, let us perhaps recall a case from 1801, of an English boy aged only 13, who was executed by hanging on the gallows at Tyburn. What was his crime? It seems that he had been condemned to die for having stolen a spoon (Westwick, 1940).

In most cases, our predecessors have either *ignored* murderousness and aggression, as in the case of Graeco–Roman infanticide, which occurred so regularly in the ancient world that it acquired an almost normative status (deMause, 1974; Kahr, 1994); or they have *punished* murderousness and destruction with retaliatory sadism, a form of unconscious identification with the aggressor. Any history of criminology will readily reveal the cruel punishments inflicted upon prisoners throughout the ages, ranging from beatings and stockades, to more severe forms of torture, culminating in eviscerations, beheadings, or lynchings.

Only during the last one hundred years have we begun to develop the capacity to respond more intelligently and more humanely to acts of dangerousness and destruction. Since the advent

of psychoanalysis, we now have access to a much deeper understanding both of the aetiology of aggressive acts and of their treatment; and nowadays we need no longer ignore criminals or abuse
them—instead, we can provide compassion and containment, as
well as conduct research that can help to prevent future acts of
violence.

The modern discipline of forensic psychotherapy, which can be
defined, quite simply, as the use of psychoanalytically orientated
"talking therapy" to treat violent, offender patients, stems directly
from the work of Sigmund Freud. Almost one hundred years ago, at
a meeting of the Vienna Psycho-Analytical Society, held on 6 February 1907, Sigmund Freud anticipated the clarion call of contemporary forensic psychotherapists when he bemoaned the often
horrible treatment of mentally ill offenders, in a discussion on the
psychology of vagrancy. According to Otto Rank, Freud's secretary
at the time, the founder of psychoanalysis expressed his sorrow at
the "nonsensical treatment of these people in prisons" (quoted in
Nunberg & Federn, 1962, p. 108).

Many of the early psychoanalysts preoccupied themselves with
forensic topics. Hanns Sachs, himself a trained lawyer, and Marie
Bonaparte, the French princess who wrote about the cruelty of war,
spoke fiercely against capital punishment. Sachs, one of the first
members of Freud's secret committee, regarded the death penalty
for offenders as an example of group sadism (Moellenhoff, 1966).
Bonaparte, who had studied various murderers throughout her
career, had actually lobbied politicians in America to free the
convicted killer Caryl Chessman, during his sentence on Death
Row at the California State Prison in San Quentin, albeit unsuccess-
fully (Bertin, 1982).

Some years later, Melanie Klein concluded her first book, the
landmark text *Die Psychoanalyse des Kindes* [*The Psycho-Analysis
of Children*], with resounding passion about the problem of violence. Mrs Klein noted that acts of criminality invariably stem from
disturbances in childhood, and that if young people could receive
access to psychoanalytic treatment at any early age, then much
cruelty could be prevented in later years. Klein expressed the hope
that: "If every child who shows disturbances that are at all severe
were to be analysed in good time, a great number of these people
who later end up in prisons or lunatic asylums, or who go completely to pieces, would be saved from such a fate and be able to
develop a normal life" (1932, p. 374).

Shortly after the publication of Klein's transformative book, Atwell Westwick, a Judge of the Superior Court of Santa Barbara, California, published a little-known though highly inspiring article, "Criminology and Psychoanalysis" (1940), in the *Psychoanalytic Quarterly*. Westwick may well be the first judge to commit himself in print to the value of psychoanalysis in the study of criminality, arguing that punishment of the forensic patient remains, in fact, a sheer waste of time. With foresight, Judge Westwick queried, "Can we not, in our well nigh hopeless and overwhelming struggle with the problems of delinquency and crime, profit by medical experience with the problems of health and disease? Will we not, eventually, terminate the senseless policy of sitting idly by until misbehavior occurs, often with irreparable damage, then dumping the delinquent into the juvenile court or reformatory and dumping the criminal into prison?" (p. 281). Westwick noted that we should, instead, train judges, probation officers, social workers, as well as teachers and parents, in the precepts of psychoanalysis, in order to arrive at a more sensitive, non-punitive understanding of the nature of criminality. He opined: "When we shall have succeeded in committing society to such a program, when we see it launched definitely upon the venture, as in time it surely will be—then shall we have erected an appropriate memorial to Sigmund Freud" (p. 281).

In more recent years, the field of forensic psychotherapy has become increasingly well constellated. Building upon the pioneering contributions of such psychoanalysts and psychotherapists as Edward Glover, Grace Pailthorpe, Melitta Schmideberg, and more recently Murray Cox, Ismond Rosen, Estela Welldon, and others too numerous to mention, forensic psychotherapy has now become an increasingly formalized discipline that can be dated to the inauguration of the International Association for Forensic Psychotherapy and to the first annual conference, held at St. Bartholomew's Hospital in London in 1991. The profession now boasts a more robust foundation, with training courses developing in the United Kingdom and beyond. Since the inauguration of the Diploma in Forensic Psychotherapy (and subsequently the Diploma in Forensic Psychotherapeutic Studies), under the auspices of the British Postgraduate Medical Federation of the University of London in association with the Portman Clinic, students can now seek further instruction in the psychodynamic treatment of patients who act out in a dangerous and illegal manner.

The volumes in this series of books will aim to provide both practical advice and theoretical stimulation for introductory students and for senior practitioners alike. In the Karnac Books Forensic Psychotherapy Monograph Series, we will endeavour to produce a regular stream of high-quality titles, written by leading members of the profession, who will share their expertise in a concise and practice-orientated fashion. We trust that such a collection of books will help to consolidate the knowledge and experience that we have already acquired and will also provide new directions for the upcoming decades of the new century. In this way, we shall hope to plant the seeds for a more rigorous, sturdy, and wide-reaching profession of forensic psychotherapy.

As the new millennium begins to unfold, we now have an opportunity for psychotherapeutically orientated forensic mental health professionals to work in close conjunction with child psychologists and with infant mental health specialists so that the problems of violence can be tackled both preventatively and retrospectively. With the growth of the field of forensic psychotherapy, we at last have reason to be hopeful that serious criminality can be forestalled and perhaps, one day, even eradicated.

References

Bertin, C. (1982). *La Dernière Bonaparte*. Paris: Librairie Académique Perrin.
deMause, L. (1974). The evolution of childhood. In: Lloyd deMause (Ed.), *The History of Childhood* (pp. 1–73). New York: Psychohistory Press.
Kahr, B. (1994). The historical foundations of ritual abuse: an excavation of ancient infanticide. In: Valerie Sinason (Ed.), *Treating Survivors of Satanist Abuse* (pp. 45–56). London: Routledge.
Klein, M. (1932). *The Psycho-Analysis of Children*, trans. Alix Strachey. London: Hogarth Press and The Institute of Psycho-Analysis. [First published as *Die Psychoanalyse des Kindes*. Vienna: Internationaler Psychoanalytischer Verlag.]
Moellenhoff, F. (1966). Hanns Sachs, 1881–1947: the creative unconscious. In: F. Alexander, S. Eisenstein, & M. Grotjahn (Eds.), *Psychoanalytic Pioneers* (pp. 180–199). New York: Basic Books.
Nunberg, H., & Federn, E. (Eds.) (1962). *Minutes of the Vienna Psychoanalytic Society. Volume I: 1906–1908*, trans. Margarethe Nunberg. New York: International Universities Press.
Westwick, A. (1940). Criminology and Psychoanalysis. *Psychoanalytic Quarterly*, 9: 269–282.

EDITOR AND CONTRIBUTORS

Dr GWEN ADSHEAD, Broadmoor Hospital, Crowthorne, Berkshire, UK.

Dr SANDRA L. BLOOM, Executive Director, The *Sanctuary*® Programs, Horsham Clinic, Ambler, Pennsylvania, and Hampton Behavioral Health Center, Rancocas, New Jersey, USA.

JOSEPH F. FODERARO, L.C.S.W., Program Director, The *Sanctuary*®, Hampton Behavioral Health Center, Rancocas, New Jersey, USA.

Dr FELICITY DE ZULUETA, Traumatic Stress Service, Maudsley Hospital, London, UK.

INTRODUCTION

In addressing the issue of violence, this volume has two main purposes. As clinicians from two countries, we come to the problem of violence primarily through the experience of our patients, who have brought to our attention the profound impact that violence has had on their lives. They have taught us much about what violence does to the body, mind, and soul of the victim, the perpetrator, and the bystander. Our first purpose is to provide practical information that will help the reader to design specific intervention strategies aimed at preventing the escalation of violence in any community.

But the study of violence has taught us that such approaches will be ineffective unless we have a coherent and meaningful framework within which to understand the continuum of violent perpetration. We have each been humbled by how little individual clinicians can do against the rising tide of violence and the legacies that violent perpetration leaves behind. We have seen that the causes of violence are multiple and yet interconnected. These causes are simultaneously medical, social,

environmental, psychological, individual, systemic, philosophical, spiritual, and political.

Only a shift in human understanding, a movement to a
higher and more integrated level of meaning, can help us to be
more effective in slowing down the pace of the disease we call
"violence". Although violence has always been an inextricable
aspect of human evolution and existence, it is clear that violent
perpetration has now become a threat to the survival of life on a
global scale. The effects of violence are infectious—they spread
down through the generations, from person to person, from
family to family, from nation to nation. And as we become more
globally interconnected, the reverberations of human rights
violations in one corner of the world are felt throughout the
entire global network.

Widespread threats to the health and well-being of broad
segments of any community require a public health approach.
A public health approach to an infectious disease is complex,
reflecting the complex nature of illness. While focusing on
efforts to identify, directly eliminate, or reduce the impact of
pathogens, public health workers simultaneously work towards
enhancing the resistance of the host as well as altering aspects
of the surroundings that make it easier for the pathogen to
flourish. For the successful eradication of disease, all of these
approaches are necessary, while none alone is sufficient.

In a public health approach, the first step is to identify the
pathogen and connect the specific pathogen with symptoms
of the disease. In the first chapter, Gwen Adshead, a psychiatrist
at Broadmoor, defines violence and shows how it manifests in
its many different forms. Her essay is a meditation on the complexity of the topic and its connection with deep human needs
and feelings. In the study of violence, most attention has been
paid to the more obvious manifestations of violent perpetration:
murder, rape, assault, and war. But we intend to elaborate on
the continuum of violence, the interconnected behaviours that
originate in patterns established in childhood and are amplified
with every successive exposure to violence.

Violence comes in many personal and social guises, and for a
public health strategy to be effective, we must understand how
the pathogen works its destruction on the host and how it

wheedles its way past the defensive system and ends up in-
filtrating and destroying healthy function. Many of the masks
of violence are accorded great social approval and accepted
as normal and even effective interpersonal strategies, but ultimately they culminate in unexpected and lethal permuta-
tions of violent perpetration. In the second chapter, Felicity
de Zulueta, Director of the Traumatic Stress Project at the
Maudsley Hospital, focuses her attention on these permuta-
tions, tracing how normal human needs, aspirations, emotions,
behaviours, and coping skills are transformed into human evils
through traumatic experience and failures of attachment.

Once we know what the pathogen is and how it works its
destruction, we have to refine methods of approach that minimize the impact of the pathogen while maintaining the integrity
of the host. Joseph Foderaro is the co-founder and program
director of *The Sanctuary*®, an inpatient treatment programme
for adults who have been first traumatized as children and usually retraumatized as adults. In this therapeutic milieu, violence
to self and violence to others are seen as opposite sides of the
same coin. The third chapter details interventions that have succeeded in approaching violence from the point of view of the
individual within an experimental short-term community that
actively practices non-violence. From a public health perspective, these efforts are directed at improving the immunity of the
host to the effects of violent perpetration. Individuals must
learn how to protect themselves from invasion, how to increase
their immunity, and how to manage infection once it has
occurred. His observations about managing violence in the
microcosm of a small inpatient unit have great utility in design-
ing strategies for the larger community as well.

The focus on the nature of the pathogenic agent and promoting the immunity of the host, while necessary, are not sufficient for an effective public health strategy. All efforts to stop
the infection of violence will fail unless we commit ourselves
to changing the social environments that are known breeding
grounds for the spread of violence—war, poverty, racism, domestic violence, child abuse, and neglect. The final chapter of this
monograph focuses on the development of "social immunity".
What steps can we take within each family, group, social service

system, social organization, or institution, and even within each relationship, to increase the resistance of the social body to violent perpetration? To suggest some answers to this question, Sandra Bloom, co-founder of *The Sanctuary* and past-President of the International Society for Traumatic Stress Studies, draws upon her experience working with victims and perpetrators of violence in the "experimental laboratory" of the inpatient setting. She extends the insights of her colleagues into the more general social realm and focuses less on the pathology of the victim or the pathology of the perpetrator and more on the pathology of the bystander. By "bystander", we refer to everyone else in the social matrix—all the rest of us who, at any point in time, are playing the role neither of victim nor of perpetrator, but are supporting or even encouraging the maintenance of social contexts within which violence is likely to happen. She will address violence as a failure of social responsibility, a failure to understand the interconnected nature of all human experience, and a symptom of widespread dysfunction of social immune systems.

The twentieth century has been called the era of "megadeath", claiming probably in excess of 175,000,000 lives as a result of deliberate, politically motivated carnage—more than the total killed in *all* previous wars, civil conflicts, and religious persecutions throughout history (Brzezinski, 1993). Although we like to pretend that violence has always been with us and is an inevitable aspect of any human endeavour, such cynicism can blind us to the escalating nature of human engagement in violence. And what has escalated can also be de-escalated, but not without enormous effort and a committed social will. Once the infection of violence has set in, it requires much more effort to undo the damage than to prevent it in the first place. We must come to understand that the human species is massively infected by violence. All of our cultural systems for making meaning are infiltrated with this lethal virus, contaminated in such a way that we now mistake the "virus" for normal "cells", for normal human feeling, acting, believing, and being. In fact, human culture has become "trauma-organized"—that is, organized around the unrecognized, unmetabolized, and untransformed thoughts, feelings, and behaviours of a post-traumatic response. We hope that this monograph can make a contribution to understanding the nature of the infection and some guidelines for managing the infection once it has set in. Ultimately, the cure lies in prevention, in stopping the intergenerational transmission of hatred, vengefulness, and pain.

VIOLENCE

CHAPTER ONE

A kind of necessity?
Violence as a public health problem

Gwen Adshead

Violence takes many forms and has appeared in many guises, especially in the twentieth century (Hobsbawm, 1994). The Oxford English Dictionary devotes three pages to definitions of violence and related words. Four separate meanings seem to emerge, which will be examined in this chapter:

1. violence as compulsion and coercion;
2. violence as extremes of feelings;
3. violence as violation;
4. violence as perversion of meaning.

Violence as compulsion and coercion: the exercise of force over others

> For they eat the bread of wickedness, and drink the wine of violence.
>
> Proverbs, 4:17

Statistics and numbers

Because so much violence goes unreported, measuring violence quantitatively is problematic. The fact that so much is hidden is a reminder that violence is often associated with secrecy and shame. Quantitatively, figures for recorded crime show a dramatic increase over the last century: for example, from 0.1 million in 1876 to nearly 6 million in 1992 in England and Wales. The same appears to be true for other European countries and the United States.

The commonest recorded crime is property theft. Violent crime (i.e. interpersonal violence) accounts for only a tiny proportion—5% to 6%—of crime. This figure is stable over time; it is a higher figure in the United States, but not dramatically so. Even if there were 100% under-reporting of all interpersonal violence, it would still represent the minority of rule-breaking behaviour in most societies.

A breakdown of the main types of violent crime committed by adults is listed in Table 1 (Barclay, Tavares, & Prout, 1995). These data suggest that even within violent crime, severe interpersonal violence is less common. Of course, the size of a problem is not an indicator of its seriousness. Furthermore, these data reflect only recorded violence, and one cannot assume that

TABLE 1.   Most common types of violent crime

serious wounding	6%
sexual offences	10%
robbery	19%
minor wounding	64%

because the wounding is described as "minor", the event did not represent a major trauma for either the victim and/or the perpetrator. Nevertheless, the comparative rarity of some types of severe interpersonal violence suggests that such violence represents a significant breakdown of functioning for the perpetrator and therefore needs to be taken extremely seriously.

The unusualness of interpersonal violence in terms of human behaviour should remind us of two things: first, that the majority of human beings do live together without violence and have the capacity to create constructive communities together. Second, that if interpersonal violence is an indicator of a derailed human interpersonal process, either at an individual or at large group level, then it has meaning for people (consciously or unconsciously) and cannot be explained as blindly instinctual.

Although interpersonal violence is unusual, it takes common forms worldwide. Some form of family violence was found in 90 societies studied by Levinson (1989). But different societies show different levels of violence. For example, Levinson indicates that while 74% of societies studied used physical punishment, only 13.3% used it regularly, and 26% used it rarely or never. Similarly Sanday (1981) found that, while 40% of societies that she studied were what she called "rape-prone", an equal proportion were not. There appears to be a significant relationship between different types of family violence—that is, if one is occurring, others are likely to be. Family violence is also affected by external factors: deprivation, unemployment, social density, and laws regulating interpersonal violence (Buchanan, 1996).

Family violence is not the only sort of interpersonal violence. It also occurs in the form of violence between strangers, either within national borders (street violence, gang wars, and civil wars) or outside (international wars). Most recorded criminal violence takes place between those who know each other, and I shall say more about this later; here I will point out only that violence between strangers tends to be a group phenomenon and involve disputes over territory and resources. In this sense, human violence resembles animal violence (Wrangham & Peterson, 1996).

Theories of violence

The literature on the origins of human violence is vast, and I shall not attempt to review it here. Theories have been generated by different disciplines such as sociology, psychology, and criminology. At different times, different theories have been more or less popular. Of late, there have been more attempts to integrate some of the theories, since it is clear that there is no one single explanation for human violence, any more than there is one for any human behaviour. The post-modern emphasis on context has forced researchers to rethink empirical strategies for studying human phenomena, and violence is an example of a phenomenon that needs multiple theoretical approaches.

Gunn (1991) lists some previous explanatory theories for violence, which he defines as "destructive aggression" (Table 2). Other reviews offer similar lists and comment that although there may be a biological substrate to aggression, its expression is profoundly affected by environmental and cultural factors.

Aggression and violence

Is aggression the same as violence? Although often presented as identical, I would like to suggest that there is an important distinction between them, as shown in Table 3.

Aggression is on a continuum with arousal, which undoubtedly is biologically mediated through complex perceptual systems in the brain and the sympathetic nervous system. There is evidence that individuals have different genetic susceptibilities to arousal, temperament, and reactivity (Kagan, 1994, 1997; Suomi, 1997). Responses to stimuli that might provoke arousal and aggression are affected by the organism's experience of anxiety which, in turn, depends on threat perception and memory (Amini et al., 1996). Threat perception is affected by previous experience of threat and its conclusion, and it is mediated by perceptual systems especially for indicators of similarity and difference. Subtle differences in the environment can signal danger; if there has been previous threat, the organism's sensitivity to those subtle differences may be increased.

TABLE 2.   Some explanatory theories of violence

violence as a human instinct	either an innate evil or a biological given
violence as a result of social frustration hypothesis	aggression as a result of frustration
social learning theory	violent behaviour is modelled, reinforced, and rewarded
social dominance theory	violence in the pursuit of power

Arousal and aggression make it possible to respond to threats to the organism's security. The recognition of similarity and difference and responses to threat are a crucial part of ordinary social survival. Presumably because of its destructive potential, aggression and arousal are organized and managed within most primate groups according to recognized and recognizable cues. In non-human primates, aggression regulates and is regulated by social hierarchies and relationships (Wrangham & Peterson, 1996). There are quite complex rules for who can bite whom and in what circumstances. Displays of aggression usually relate to competition for food, partners, or social position.

Human aggression is regulated in a much more complex and elaborate way. A degree of aggression is necessary for motivated functioning and is highly regulated within certain rules, regulations, and boundaries. Although there may be social and cultural differences about the rules between different societies, aggression is still regulated, and its creative possibilities are maintained. The most obvious example is in relation to sport,

TABLE 3.   Distinctions between concepts

arousal	threat perception, sympathetic arousal
aggression	includes competition; a "fight" type of arousal
violence	aggression that exceeds a containing boundary

where competition is a highly regulated way of expressing aggression, both by individuals and by groups.

Violence occurs when the internal and external boundaries for aggression are broken. A sporting example makes the point. Mr Tyson and Mr Holyfield are professional boxers. By boxing rules, Mr Tyson is *allowed* to assault Mr Holyfield physically within certain boundaries, even to the extent of knocking him unconscious and causing him brain damage. He is even *allowed* to kill him by hitting him. He is not, however, allowed to bite his ear off.

Boundaries, rules, and thresholds

The absurdity of the Holyfield/Tyson fight reveals a very human preoccupation with rules of behaviour. The best example of this is war and the "rules of engagement". Hobsbawm (1997) argues that traditional wars, in this sense, were aggressive but not violent; that professional fighting does not involve feelings of interpersonal hatred but utilizes aggression within certain aims to achieve a certain (usually territorial) purpose. He suggests that contemporary wars are based on hatred and the demonization of the opponent, which then justifies attacks on civilians and non-combatants. He is thus making a distinction between organized conflict that is aggressive and barbaric conflict that is violent.

The literature seems to suggest that there can be aggression without violence, but not violence without aggression—that is, violence occurs when there is a breaching of the internal and external boundaries that control aggression and arousal. The question, then, is how and where the boundaries are set. Using Belsky's (1980) ecological model, we may postulate that boundary-setting for aggression takes place at four levels (see Table 4). Individual risks for violence at Level 1 (genetic susceptibility to arousal and fragile temperament) may interact with stressors in the family and social system (Level 2). The family is influenced by stressors mediated by Level 3 structures. Both Level 2 and Level 3 are influenced by Level 4 factors—for example, cultural attitudes to violence towards children. The extent to which

TABLE 4. Boundaries

Level 1	the inner world of the individual: including biological make-up and the capacity for self-reflection
Level 2	the microsystem of the individual in social and family context: including the person's attachment and relationship history
Level 3	the exosystem of the community: legal and economic strategies that influence the environment
Level 4	the macrosystem: including the cultural matrix of the society, international relations, and the management of difference

Level 4 and Level 1 might continuously influence one another in a type of feedback loop is unknown.

For each society, we can explore where the threshold for violence lies and how it changes over time. The key message is that we are not helpless pawns of internal drives but, rather, that the boundaries are set where we want them to be. This means that all individuals and groups may be involved in complex ethical decision-making processes. For example, Gunn (1991) argues that some types of violence (like wars) are of benefit to society, although such a benefit would have to be set against any social costs. Groups and individuals might also have to consider the social importance of never treating others "merely" as a means—Kant's categorical imperative.

Victims of violence

The experience and needs of victims are described in depth by my colleagues in this volume, and I shall make only two points here. First, criminal victimization is a relatively common experience: recent surveys of Western populations show that one person in four has been a victim of one or more crime (Barclay, Tavares, & Prout, 1995). The highest rates for victimization seem to be in the most "civilized" places: Australia, New Zealand, and the United States, where the Department of Justice reports that 83% of the population has experienced victimization. Victims of crime tend to be the disenfranchised and vulnerable— uneducated young men, ethnic minorities, children, the elderly.

The second point relates to the experience of victimization as a risk factor for later violence (see de Zulueta, this volume). Physical abuse in childhood increases the chance of arrest for a violent offence in adulthood in men (Widom & Ames, 1994; Weiler & Widom, 1996); it also increases the risk of developing anti-social personality disorder (APD), which is, by definition, associated with criminal and violent behaviour (Luntz & Widom, 1994). Although the cycle of violence is not a perfect circle (Widom, 1989), addressing the needs of the victimized may be an important part of any strategy for violence reduction.

Violence as extremes of feeling

Why, I can smile, and murder while I smile

Shakespeare, *Richard III*

Different types of violence

One of the central assumptions of this chapter is that all human action has meaning. However, understanding the meaning of violence is complex, because violence is heterogeneous and contextual. Various types of violence are listed in Table 5.

Violence that is in the context of a relationship, and violence that is not

Most violence occurs between people who know each other well (Boyd, 1994; Barclay, Tavares, & Prout, 1995). Of murdered women, 88% are killed by those they know, and often those they love or have loved; the same is true for 69% of murdered men. Of raped women, 66% know the man who rapes them; again, often these are men with whom they have had a relationship in the past. The presence of mental illness may increase the risk of assault on strangers, although even here, family mem-

TABLE 5. Various types of violence

- violence in the context of relationships and violence to strangers
- useful violence and useless violence
- violence by individuals and violence by groups
- violence by men and violence by women
- violence by children and violence by adults
- violence by those who are mentally ill
- repeated violence to strangers

bers, especially mothers, are most at risk from the mentally ill who commit homicide (Boyd, 1994; Estroff, Zimmer, Lachicotte, & Benoit, 1994).

The same applies at a large group level. Although wars may be seen as violence between strangers, most wars are between brother states or neighbouring societies—consider the Arab/Israeli wars, the Iran/Iraq war, and civil conflict in Northern Ireland and Bosnia, where neighbours attacked one another. In contrast to organized aggression, violence between family members or intimates does not seem to have "rules of engagement", so that family violence is frequently extreme and uncontrolled. It is likely that such "rules" are more difficult to construct in those situations where there is profound emotional attachment.

Useful violence and useless violence

There are types of violence that are instrumental for some other purpose, and others that are not. Examples of the first type include some types of rape (Knight & Prentky, 1990), in which violence is used to subjugate the victim but does not appear to be an end in itself. Sadism may be an example of violence that is an end in itself, although it is perhaps noteworthy that most sadists are actually aroused by fantasies of domination and submission rather than by the inflicting of pain as such. Torture is also an instrumental form of violence and perhaps a rare example of violence without aggression—or, at least, minimal aggression in some circumstances. Torture is generally carried out by civic agents and is licensed at a state level (even where it is officially denied)—another good example of how violence is an expression of boundary setting at small and large group levels.

The concept of "useless violence" is one used by Primo Levi (1989) to describe the violence suffered by Nazi death- and work-camp victims. He describes violence beyond torture or sadism, which appears to have only the purpose of humiliation and the destruction of identity. Given the importance of identity to survival (Bettelheim, 1960) and the purpose of the Nazi death-camps, the violence was perhaps not so useless after all.

Violence by individuals and violence by groups

As suggested above, violence by groups tends to take place against strangers. In this sense, strangers are those who are perceived to be different to the group norm. In this context, one thinks of gay-bashing, gang rape, lynching, and gang warfare.

Biologically, small groups are vital to human survival, so the construction of groups and the maintenance of their boundaries is vital to reduce anxiety. By locating difference outside the group, group aggression to strangers strengthens the group identity by promoting cohesion and reducing the risk of internal splits (Agazarian, 1994). Unfortunately, such cohesion as a result of violence is usually short-lived because the group is fundamentally insecure, and further violence will be necessary to maintain the status quo. Violent groups—especially family groups—are likely to be anxious, with diminished capacities for self-containment: the experience of the Corleone family in "The Godfather" makes the point.

The dynamics of violence between individuals are not dissimilar to the dynamics of group violence. In the case of domestic violence, a man and a woman form an insecure attachment. Attachment relationships operate at the boundary between two people's personal identities. Where there has been insecure attachment, the batterer may be confused about the boundary between himself and his victim. Cultural constructs of dependent people as possessions also help to blur the distinction between perpetrator and victim. Because the batterer may see no boundary between his identity and that of his partner, any threat she makes to leave causes crippling anxiety by threatening an internal sense of self-cohesion. As anxiety begins to rise, positive interpersonal bonds are shattered, and those closest become the receptacles for fearful projections. However, in pair relationships the other person is also necessary for the containment of the anxiety, so there is a double blow.

In the face of such anxiety, the boundary between thought, word, and action is quickly crossed, and the batterer controls by violence. This brings relief; however, this can only be temporary, since the batterer does not have internal security and the violence will happen again. This cycle can be seen in slightly different forms in child abusers—and especially in female child abusers. Violence also increases self-esteem in the perpetrator (Rosen, 1989), in a way that is similar to the sense of group esteem and cohesion described above.

Violence by women and violence by men

There is no place in the world where men make up less than 80% of people arrested for violence—now or at any time in history (Monahan, 1997, note 32). Thus women who do act violently are rare and unusual, and they cause more anxiety than do their male counterparts. In the United Kingdom, services for women offenders—especially those who suffer from mental illness—are poor (Adshead & Morris, 1995; Dell, Robertson, James, & Grounds, 1993).

Rather than emphasizing the differences, it may be illuminating to look at the similarities between male and female offenders. Although violence by women is often associated with mental illness (Wilczynski, 1997), there is little empirical evidence to bear this out. Of those female offenders who are diagnosed, personality disorder is by far the most common, as it is for perpetrators of both sexes. Personality disorder diagnoses are associated with histories of childhood deprivation and abuse, and both male and female offenders have such histories. In surveys, the prevalence of reported childhood abuse does tend to be higher for female offenders; however, this may reflect only that women tend to be more likely to respond to questions about neurotic symptoms, and men may be reluctant to disclose histories of abuse.

Both male and female offenders tend to attack those they know well, especially partners and children. Women are perhaps more likely to attack their children physically, although most sexual abuse is carried out by male carers. Women may attack children because they are closest to them (cf. attacks on parents by adults) and because children are vulnerable in a way that adult partners are not. Violent perpetrators preferentially target the vulnerable, and for most women this is likely to be their own or other people's children. Women are also attached to their children in a way that men may not be because of the history of physical attachment between them (Welldon, 1988); an attack on a child may represent, to a mother, an attack on herself. Once again, we can see how violence can occur where there is a failure to recognize a boundary and that boundary is breached.

Both male and female perpetrators can act cruelly to their victims, although sadistic cruelty tends to be the province of a small subset of offenders. Both men and women can act violently in groups or in pairs. Lynch mobs may be mixed in sex, and violence to individuals may be carried out by mixed pairs who may be in a relationship. In such cases, it may be that the violence acts as a bond between the offenders and maintains the relationship. In this context, it is noteworthy that the presence of a friend or a partner may help to make the commission of violence more acceptable to either perpetrator. Gitta Sereny describes this mechanism as one used by the Nazis, who used to put friends and colleagues together to carry out violence (Sereny, 1974).

There are clearly similarities between male and female offenders. But it might be said that the difference in absolute numbers and proportions of offenders is too great to dismiss. The explanation is likely to involve a mixture of factors, of which biology may well be the least important. What seems to be of much greater importance is gender role. Young women are socialized from an early age to be submissive and non-confrontational and to manage their aggression in quite a different way from young men. Their experience of adolescence may well be different (Brown & Gilligan, 1992), so that their identity comes to be bound up with their connection to other people. This may reduce a sense of agency at one level and promote connection with others at another, so that boundary maintenance may come more easily to young women. Victimization experience may also leave a high proportion of young women with diminished self-esteem; however, victimization may also be a risk factor for violence, so the effect is complex. One way of looking at this may be to assume that women can act just as violently as do men in similar circumstances, it just "takes more" (Robins, 1986). The parallel question might be to ask why it seems to take so much less for men, and to ask, further, whether males are more violent because culturally they are "allowed" to be so.

Violence by children and violence by adults

Violence by children is rare, and is thus shocking when it occurs. Violent children tend to attack either caretakers or those they know, and family members are most at risk. If strangers are attacked, the mechanism seems to be similar for violence by adults: a vulnerable victim is selected—usually a much younger child. Most child perpetrators are not mentally ill, but they may come from backgrounds that are deprived, neglectful, or abusive.

Violence by those who are mentally ill and those who are not

It should be clear by now that violence is generally carried out by those who are mentally well, in terms of formal diagnoses, such as schizophrenia. The data also suggest that most mentally ill people are never violent. However, recent research suggests that some types of mental illness carry an increased risk of violence to others (Monahan & Steadman, 1994). Violence is associated with paranoid states of mind and with active paranoid psychotic symptoms, such as hallucinations and delusions; delusions of threat to personal identity—such as "he is putting thoughts into my mind"—are particularly associated with violence (Link & Stueve, 1994).

It seems from the data that violence by the mentally ill has a kind of rationality, as suggested by Link and Stueve. Mentally ill offenders are often frightened by their victims, believing them to be interfering with that most crucial of possessions: their identity. A paranoid state of mind implies an individual who is highly aroused, anxious, and afraid. Psychotic symptoms may affect both threat perception and the ability to judge safety. Medication that reduces anxiety and arousal may help to increase a patient's sense of safety, as may admission to hospital.

In conclusion, it might be argued that the very act of violence is an indicator of mental illness—that crime is a type of disease. This view has been debated at length, especially in the courts, where the distinction between "ordinary" badness and "ill" badness is crucial in terms of apportioning blame. The distinction is an important one, and it is influenced by ideas about free will (Bavidge, 1989). Diagnostically speaking, the majority of violent offenders are not mentally ill; however, it would be fair to say that nearly all violent offenders are people who are often in disturbed and distressed states of mind. Despair, loneliness, and envy are not mental illnesses, but they are potent stressors, and it is rare to find a "happy" perpetrator of violence. Given the frequency of histories of childhood abuse and violence, it is perhaps not surprising to find that offenders have disturbed patterns of relating to others and, presumably, to themselves (van IJzendoorn et al., 1997; Fonagy et al., 1997).

Repeated violence to strangers

Here I refer to the literature on serial killers and rapists. Serial rapists appear to be men who hate women and for whom all women are interchangeable. Many serial rapists also kill their victims, and the literature seems to suggest that ritualized control is important to such offenders. (The interested reader is referred to Wilson & Seaman, 1990, or to Lunde & Sigal, 1990.) It may be important to emphasize that serial killers are probably comparatively rare. The borderline between mental distress and mental illness is paper-thin for such offenders, and the offending behaviour may be a defence against severe mental illness. Whatever may be the meaning for the offender, it seems that at some level the offender feels justified in what he does. This justification will have its roots in the offender's Level 1 and Level 2 experience (see above). It is difficult not to think that such men are also affected by Level 3 and Level 4 processes, so that, for example, those men who preferentially attack and rape/kill women have attitudes that support the idea of "woman" as ultimately one who can be legitimately treated in this way (Smith, 1989).

The feelings associated with violence

There is a stereotypical fantasy of the so-called "cold-blooded" offender: one who can hurt and never flinch. Levi describes such men and women in his work. But in practice such offenders are rare. Since the genesis of violence lies in human feelings and relationships combined with insufficient thought, I think it unlikely that violence can take place without the offender having strong feelings about it. The extent to which such feelings are hidden, even from the offender himself, are of course another matter. Lifton (1986) describes how those doctors involved in selections for death in the death-camps were almost permanently drunk every evening; one can only imagine how much of their internal worlds they had to anaesthetize.

Man is a communicator: those 2% of genes that separate us from our primate brothers contain within them—amongst other things—an enormous capacity for speech and symbolic representation, so that thought can be transcribed and developed into communication. Where words fail, man is left with feelings that need to be processed because they are intolerable. Thought is necessary for words, and where thought fails, there may be action without thought. This is especially true of negative feelings—shame (J. Gilligan, 1997), anger, fear, grief, and revenge.

> I pray thee, do on them some violent death
> They have been violent to me and mine
>
> [Shakespeare, *Titus Andronicus*, V.ii.108–109]

Where the feelings that an individual experiences relate to a person's sense of identity, the urge to communicate is high. People need not only to know who they are—they need to let others know and to be in connection with others. It is only through being in connection with others that one's identity is given life, by being recognized by another. The dangers of the loss of personal identity were awfully demonstrated by the repeated description of those in the Nazi death-camps, often called by other inmates "the Musselmen". These were men and women whose despair attacked their very identity as people, so that when they gave up trying to preserve their lives, they lost their personal identity. This psychological death of identity seems to have hastened their biological death, according to witnesses (Levi, 1989). Thus the stakes attached to the possession of an internal sense of self are high. For many offenders, the violence occurs in response to a literally "unspeakable" sense of nothingness internally;

> I took a life because I needed one. [Cox, 1973, p. 96]

Violence can be seen as a means of keeping the self together and preventing disintegration, and the feelings that go with that disintegration. It is not too fanciful to see national violence as operating the same mechanism. Violence that controls dissidents is controlling internal state anxiety and fears that the state will disintegrate. Something of this "identity crisis" was apparent in South Africa before the new regime; it was also apparent in the former Yugoslavia.

> I think that people act violently because they don't have a voice. [Quote from a patient in a maximum-security hospital]

An inability to express feelings in words is called alexithymia. One of the first steps in the therapy of violent offenders is to give them a voice and to help to provide them with language. Until there is language, the ability to think is restricted, and there can be little connection between offenders and the large group of connections from which their offending cuts them off.

Violence as violation: to break up

Richard loves Richard; that is, I am I.
Is there a murderer here?
No. Yes.
I am. Then fly.
What? From myself?

Shakespeare, *Richard III*, V.iii.185–187

Violence and identity: Richard III

I would now like to look at the way violence can contribute to personal identity. In *Richard III*, Shakespeare has constructed a man whose whole identity is uncertain from the beginning, and it is somehow crystallized by violence. He first appears as one of the Duke of York's three sons, with nothing to mark him out except a marked physical handicap, which renders him unattractive. There is some suggestion that he is especially close to his father; certainly, he does not seem popular with his mother.

As the plays unfold (in *Henry VI, Part III*, and *Richard III*), it becomes clear that Richard feels both unlovable and unloving:

I have no brother, I am like no brother
since I cannot be a lover . . .,
I am determined to prove a villain, and hate. . . .

[*Richard III*, I.i.28–30]

His identity is delineated by violence, both internally and externally, as it obtains him new names in the form of titles and, ultimately, a new identity as king. This identity, however, is no firmer than the others; not only does Richard constantly fear that someone will threaten his monarchy as he himself was a threat, but his own internal sense of identity is clearly an anxious one, as the quote suggests. He cannot keep attachments, even to past friends; ultimately, the night before his most important battle for survival, he suffers intrusive memories of his past violence. He is deserted by his army, defeated, and killed. Something of these same mechanisms were at work in Nazi Germany, and the same violence went into the creation of the identities of some of the major figures in Hitler's government—those of Goering and Goebbels in particular.

Violence and masculine identity

The gender difference in relation to violence raises the question of whether violence is an essential feature of masculine identity. Female gender role, and the whole concept of "femininity", is a construction that includes both positive and negative attributes (Showalter, 1987). Positive attributes include sensitivity and the capacity to nurture; negative attributes include submission, passivity, and lack of agency—that is, an inability to make choices and take action. In contrast, the concept "masculine" has attributes that include domination, assertion, and agency, and perhaps especially the attribute of "not-being" feminine (see Table 6).

Personal identity is closely linked with social gender role construct (Attanucci, 1988). Since the normal expression of human aggression will result in feelings of dominance, assertion, and agency, it is difficult not to think that women's personal identity requires them to over-control their aggression and

TABLE 6.   Gender role constructs

the construct "feminine"	weak, passive, helpless, submissive, unassertive, lacking in agency
the construct "masculine"	strong, active, assertive, dominant, able to act and make choices

men's identity requires them to under-control their aggression, so increasing their risk of violence.

The difficulty with this gender role split is two-fold. First, it is not possible for any human to feel dominant, assertive, and full of agency all the time. Childhood is the most obvious time for dependent and passive feelings, but illness and old age are others. Stressful life changes, such as sudden bereavement or loss of employment, are also times when individuals feel powerless and lack agency. The key point is that such dependency feelings are normal and necessary; they are not a problematic set of feelings that have to be located in the weakest group.

The second problem with this affective split by sex is that it not only puts men at increased risk of acting violently—the act of violence then becomes linked to the sense of self and masculine identity. To feel dependent, passive, or powerless may for a man be an attack on his sense of identity, not only as a person, but also as a man, causing massive unconscious anxiety. Nancy Chodorow (1994) has suggested that a boy has to forge a new identity separate from that of his mother, whereas a girl can retain an identity with that of her mother, by virtue of a physical identity. Forging a new identity may not be problematic if there is strong paternal identity with which a boy can identify. The paternal role is one where masculinity can be combined with caring for others; it seems likely that successful maternal and paternal activities are not actually very different (M. Lamb, 1997).

However, boys may have problems when they feel a need to separate from their mothers but have only a violent or an absent father with whom to identify. Fatherhood has been a role that has not been the subject of research until comparatively recently, particularly in the context of family violence (Sternberg, 1997). Given that we know that many violent offenders have had histories of childhood violence, either by witness or direct victimization, it may be that when they were boys, those men had had only a violent father with whom to identify (cf. Fraiberg, Adelson, & Shapiro, 1980). The social construction of masculinity will require victimized boys to deny the victim aspect of their identity in terms of real feelings and experiences. It suggests to them that to pay attention to those feelings of fear or distress is to negate their male identity—to "die" as a man. The same is true even if these boys were exposed to a violent mother, since in such circumstances the father is likely to be either psychologically or physically absent or, possibly, equally violent.

So the social construct of masculinity poses an existential problem for the boy who has witnessed or experienced victimization, let alone normal dependency needs. He feels fear, anxiety, and need, and is therefore a "woman". But he is not a woman—so what is he? Anxiety follows, combined with an urgent need to establish a male identity. The only identifying figure is a violent one, which denies the existence of his dependency feelings. He must therefore deny and "kill off" a part of himself, thus attacking his own sense of identity. The masculine construct seems to offer a confirmatory role, but it cannot address the underlying sense of threat to identity. The "not-male" feelings will have their life and expression, but they cannot be thought about or spoken—they will have to be acted upon or projected. The social role puts an abused man at risk of acting violently the moment a stressor appears that rekindles the dependency feelings.

The validity of gender role constructions

The polarity of affective life implied by the constructs "masculine" and "feminine" is unrealistically polarized and represents an impossible task for either sex to achieve. Pursuit of these role ideals must result in failure, since some degree of aggression is good for all humans in certain circumstances, and no human can live without dependency needs for others. Failure at gender role enactment produces anxiety as it threatens personal identity, but anxiety will stimulate dependency needs, and so the cycle of failure continues. As I have suggested above, the cycle becomes more vicious where men have additional and extreme experiences of violence and victimization during their childhood and adolescence.

The question is why it continues. Why is it culturally necessary for one group of people to be submissive? Why should one group of people need to feel powerful all the time and at the same time not be allowed to feel powerless, even though such a state is inevitable from time to time? The constructs are not apparently biologically or culturally workable.

Historically, constructs like this, which divide communities, have been successful ways for those communities to live, albeit at a cost. This cost is paid by the vulnerable, who are used as tension-relievers by those others who feel violent as a result of their anxiety. If the potentially violent people are slightly more powerful than their victims, then those victims will be seen as legitimate targets. If hatred of dependency is culturally con- structed on top of those gender roles, then the community that is created accepts disparities in power as bad luck and vio- lence to the less powerful as more bad luck for the victims. The answer is for the victim to become more powerful: so you hit me with a fist, I hit you with a stick; you shoot me with a small gun, I get a bigger one; you get your friends to help, I raise an army. Dependency is a signal that you are a victim, and that it is your fault for being so.

That dependence and vulnerability are denigrated in west- ern culture is most obvious in relation to the needs of those who deal with society's traumatic events. The macho culture in the uniformed services has traditionally made it impossible for men who develop post-traumatic stress disorder (PTSD) in the line of duty to get help. The denigration of dependency becomes the denigration of tenderness and attachment, so that emotional intimacy and erotic feelings become an arena for violence. No type of sex but physical penetration is "real"; there is no culmi- nation of sex without male ejaculation. Rape is an assault on the physical and erotic identity of the victim, so that both male and female victims say, "I feel dirty inside".

Victims of any crime are often made to feel both responsible and ashamed of their pain and fear. John Boorman's film, "De- liverance", was almost not released for public view because the agonies of being a victim of sexual assault were thought too dreadful for audiences to see. Contrast this with the hundreds of films that depict violence from the point of view of the perpe- trator: we can see what it is to be a rapist, not a victim. It is perhaps noteworthy that the victim in "Deliverance" was male.

Finally, we may consider what it means when a sophisticated British literary and political magazine, which has been in print for over 100 years, prints an editorial that suggests that bullying is good for people and builds up their "moral character" ("Editorial: Mr. Cook's Cruelty", *The Spectator*, 17 May 1997).

Violence as perversion of meaning: the importance of language

Do not lie, and do not do what you hate, for all things are manifest before Heaven.

For there is nothing hidden that shall not be revealed, and there is nothing covered that shall remain without being uncovered.

The Gospel According to Thomas, v. 18–20,
Guillamont et al., 1959

Throughout this chapter, I have suggested that actions have meaning, that violent actions occur when thought and speech fail, and that the violent need to be helped to find speech. However, all speech has meaning too, and I will suggest that there are ways that violence can be expressed by perverting the meaning of language. In this section, I look at how the use of language contributes to a culture of violence and legitimates it.

Denial and the minimization of violence

Violence may be a defence against shame (J. Gilligan, 1997) but, sadly, one that is fragile. All too often the shameful feelings break through, with accompanying feelings of guilt, distress, and grief. For those not pushed beyond the physical boundary of violence, psychological denial becomes an important part of living with violence.

The extent of the denial by offenders is huge, especially in relation to interpersonal violence. Adversarial systems of justice, which pit the word of the alleged victim against the word of the alleged perpetrator (such as the U.S. and U.K. criminal justice systems) presume innocence until guilt is proved. This means that even offenders who know that they are guilty may protest their innocence and deny their offence. This is particularly true of sex offenders (Kennedy & Grubin, 1992; Salter, 1988). Denial of sex crimes may also be influenced by offenders' beliefs about gender role stereotypes. Interestingly, most homicide perpetrators admit their violence, especially in cases of family homicide.

An adversarial system in law and a legal presumption of innocence are clearly important protections against infringements of liberty and the risk of false accusation. However, in the case of family and sexual violence, the criminal justice process compounds high levels of denial. There is some reason to think that sexual and family violence is not taken seriously by the courts: a newspaper reported recently that a conviction for domestic violence is no bar to promotion within the British police force. Consider also the case of a young woman held hostage in her bedroom by burglars and buggered with a hammer. Her assailants were caught, tried, and convicted: they could only be convicted of indecent assault at that time because buggery was not considered as serious as rape. Their sentence for the burglary was longer than the sentence for the assault, and the judge stated in passing that "the victim suffered no great trauma".

Denial clearly occurs also at a large-group level. The defendants at the Nuremberg trials (both medical and non-medical) struggled to admit that what they had done was wrong. Gitta Sereny (1994) in her masterful biography of Albert Speer eloquently describes how an educated and civilized man struggled to acknowledge the extent of the violence to which he had been party. Throughout his life after the war, he seems to have danced with the possibility of knowing what he did. Perhaps the knowledge would have been too awful to tolerate, too inconsistent with his own self-identity. That the stakes for knowledge are high is amply demonstrated in Sereny's biography of Franz Stangl, commandant at Treblinka, who was responsible for the deaths of over 500,000 people. In her interviews with him, he could scarcely acknowledge his guilt; when he finally did so, he died 19 hours later:

I think he died because he had finally however briefly faced
himself and told the truth. . . . the moment when he became
the man he should have been. [Sereny, 1974, p. 366[1]]

The disappearance of the perpetrator
from the language

In writing about violence, it is possible for the perpetrator to
vanish from the language, leaving only the victim at the scene
of the crime. Attention then focuses on the victim and on the
victim's part in the events that lead up to the violence. S. Lamb
(1990) describes how professional reports about wife-batterers
rarely refer to the offenders at all and tend to describe the violence in a passive voice (see Table 7 for an example). Thus the
perpetrator's deliberate choice to act brutally is omitted, and
the victim's experience is only reported in a passive voice. Note
too that it was the blows and not the man who caused the
bruising in (b).

The violence literature has focused on the needs of victims in
a way that has allowed the offenders to "escape". The focus of
attention—and to some extent the responsibility for dealing
with the problem of violence—is once again left with the victim.
Researchers (with a few honourable exceptions) seem to have
focused on questions about the victim's mental state, not the
perpetrator's (Table 8).

Even at theoretical levels language is important in relation to
violence and interpersonal relationships: for example, in relation to models of ethical reasoning (C. Gilligan, 1982). Traditional ethical theory has tended to be rights-based, focusing on
the importance of autonomy. Violence to others is wrong because it violates the right to be left alone. Alternative models

TABLE 7. Describing battering

NOT	(a)	"he beat her repeatedly, causing severe facial bruising"
BUT	(b)	"she experienced repeated blows, which left severe facial bruising"

TABLE 8. Victim focus

NOT	"Why is he doing that"? and "Why doesn't he stop?"
BUT	"Why doesn't she leave?"

emphasize the relationships between human persons and see these relationships as the matrix from which ethical considerations come. Violence in this sense is a breach of a duty not to harm others and also a breach of a connection between the victim and the offender.

Disturbing the universe: the "just world" theory

Workers with offenders and victims can sometimes see each other as adversaries, with each one being seen as "for" either the victim or the perpetrator. After five years of working with offenders, I went to work in a service for victims. After two months, a former colleague suggested to me that now I was "on the side of the victim", implying that I could not possibly deal with an offender patient fairly. This polarity of victim and offender identity, so reminiscent of the gender-role split described above, prevents both sets of professionals from seeing how much victims and offenders have in common.

Having said that perpetrators and victims have much in common, there is a caveat. This caveat reflects a moral valence to work with the violent and the victims of violence, which is unlike other types of psychotherapeutic work. Generally, psychotherapeutic work is required to be non-judgemental: lack of censure and total acceptance of the individual are among the curative factors of any psychological therapy. But can we be non-judgemental where there has been real breaching of a moral boundary? Violence is a breaching of an ethical boundary as surely as it breaches psychological, legal, and social boundaries. As members of the civic community, large and small, we all contribute to the construction and formation of ethical boundaries through our relationships with each other. An attack on one is an attack on all of us. It is therefore not possible for the therapist to be exempt from the ethical process. Although the victim and offender identities are intertwined, they are separate and must not be confused:

> I do not know and it does not much interest me to know whether in my depths, there lurks a murderer, but I do know that I was a guiltless victim and I was not a murderer. [Primo Levi, 1989]

It would be much more comforting if all victims had in some way contributed to their abuse—so reassuring if they could be allocated equal responsibility. This would support the notion of a "just world" (Janoff-Bulman & Frieze, 1983), where bad things only happen to bad people and the righteous are safe. The shattering of beliefs about the existence of a just world is one of the devastating sequelae faced by survivors of victimization; for some, it may take a lifetime. ·

The "just world" theory is important to offenders too. Many offenders make it possible to hurt others by making them into offenders and thus justifying the use of violence against them. The most common example lies in the violence used by men towards wives who are leaving them. It is noteworthy that the defence of provocation in English law accepts that a man may do extreme violence to his wife if she "offends" by adultery or departure. However, the realization that the victim was not an offender and did not "deserve" what happened, and that the offender has in fact made the universe "unjust", is a disturbing one for many offenders, and one that takes a great deal of time to understand and accept. Given the awfulness of this realization, it is understandable that it takes men a long time to admit their responsibility (Cox, 1990), and they may need a great deal of help before they can do so.

A discourse of possession

One of the biggest language problems relates to notions of possession. Given that it is apparently acceptable to damage things and not people, violent offenders tend to reduce their victims to the status of things and to talk about them in that way. This happens most commonly in relation to family members (children, wives, domestic animals), but it is also a recognizable mechanism in wars and in interpersonal violence by strangers. The dehumanization of the victim (Storr, 1968) seems to be an important precursor to violent action against the victim—another way of making it "all right" for the offender.

The belief that people possess each other can be a primitive defence against the real existential pain of attachments. No attachment lasts forever, and to engage in a meaningful attachment is always to be at risk of pain at its inevitable loss. No one is in our control, especially not the people we love most. Another equivalent is our inability ever to know the mind of another: no one's mind can be known or owned by us, hence the importance of St Paul's assurance:

then I shall know, even as I am known

[1 Corinthians 13]

The literature makes it clear that most violence takes place at a time of threatened separation (Bowlby, 1984). Violent people want to control the victim's mind and heart. Their inability to do so is a painful reminder that attachment means loss, and that pain later is part of the present joy of any attachment (Lewis, 1963). An extreme example is provided by one of Britain's few serial killers, who killed his victims to stop them from leaving him (Masters, 1986).

Finally, our concern about violence in the context of beliefs about possession must extend to the protection of the planet and our environment. We know that physical environments contribute to the genesis of violence (Cooke, 1991); how much greater may the risk of future violence worldwide be if all the beautiful environments are destroyed. It costs little to plan for green spaces in new towns; it is dangerous to destroy the biological environment of which we are a part. Somehow we need to put our relationship with the earth and its non-human inhabitants on a different footing, one not based on possession but on mutual benefit.

Conclusion: things to do, and things not to do

> Both the victim and the oppressor need refuge and
> protection
>
> Primo Levi, 1989

Recently, two psychiatrists described the conditions they believed encouraged violence to flourish. These are set out in Tables 9 and 10.

The similarity between these two lists is striking. Both authors emphasize that the construction and perpetuation of rigid hierarchies, based on difference that is seen as unchangeable, makes for a civic structure that is unstable: inequality is insecurity. Rather than promoting difference, we need to be trying to find the connections and similarities between each other.

In classical game theory, the prisoner's dilemma explores the advantages and disadvantages of mutual cooperation. Let-

TABLE 9. Conditions for a culture of violence

1   punishing people ever more harshly

2   legalizing drugs—such as alcohol—that stimulate violence and criminalizing drugs with little direct effect, thus constructing a "war" on drugs, which diverts money away from real causes of violence

3   increase disparity and sense of shame between rich and poor

4   deprive poor of access to education

5   perpetuate caste divisions in society

6   provide entertainment that glorifies violence [and shows its effects only from the aggressor's perspective]

7   make lethal weapons available

8   maximize polarity between the social roles of the genders

9   encourage prejudice against homosexuality

10   legitimize corporal punishment and physical violence to children

11   control economy in such a way that unemployment is never abolished or even minimized.

From J. Gilligan, 1996.

TABLE 10. How to destroy a sense of community

1	encourage large status differentials: dominance increases where there is competition for resources
2	diminish the potential for reciprocal altruism
3	ignore the needs of the weakest, including attention as well as material goods
4	never smile

From Holmes, 1996.

ting someone down once may win in the short term; but where there is memory and connection over time, then cooperation and power-sharing is a better strategy, and a more stable one. "Having a friend help" leads to reduced violence in schools (Korkenderfer & Ladd, 1997) and could usefully extend outside the playground.

Cecil Day Lewis (1947) describes love as "a kind of necessity". Perhaps violence too is a kind of necessity while people's needs for love and personal connection remain unfulfilled. It seems certain that violence is a universal language that we all can speak at certain times and in certain situations.

Note

1. I am grateful to Gitta Sereny for permitting me to quote from *Into That Darkness*.

CHAPTER TWO

Violent attachments and attachment to violence

Felicity de Zulueta

V iolence is a preventable disease. Many of its causes and effects are now known to us, and in many cases they are preventable—so why do we have such a problem in dealing with it? This is the subject of this chapter.

Cultural traditions of violence in Western family life

Family violence—the hidden epidemic

The horrifying stories of murder, child abuse, rape, and torture that we see on television and read about on an almost daily basis are but the tip of the iceberg. The figures in the United Kingdom are not generally as high as those in the United States, but violence is also becoming more of a problem in this country. In the United Kingdom the homicide rate in 1991 was 5.5 for every 100,000 citizens (Ellis, 1992). The cause of this epidemic lies mainly in the secret violence of family life—a hidden violence our society does its best to ignore.

We know that women and children are more likely to be abused, threatened, and even killed by members of their own family than by anybody else. The traditional male head of the family is usually the agent of that violence.

In one English survey carried out in London, one in three women said that she had been punched, slapped, kicked, or head-butted, and that she had suffered attempted strangulation or been struck by a weapon—many of these attacks resulting in injury. Nearly two out of every three men interviewed said that they would use violence on their partners in a "conflict" situation that might be as minor as not having dinner ready on time (McCarney, 1996).

Women are likely to experience violence in approximately one in four marriages (Bakowski, Murch, & Walker, 1983). From these figures, we can see that violence perpetrated by men on their partners accounts for nearly a quarter of all reported violence and for over 70% of violence in the home. These figures may well distort the real levels of violence, since family violence often takes place in secrecy: one in four of the women questioned had told no one, and even fewer had reported violence to the police (Dobash & Dobash, 1980). As for rape, about one and a half million wives or ex-wives have been the victims of rape in the United Kingdom (Dyer, 1990). Domestic violence can also have fatal results: in the United Kingdom two women are murdered every week by their husbands or lovers (Lees, 1977).

Research in the United States shows a clear link between physical and sexual abuse (Finkelhor, 1983). In homes where marital abuse occurs, child abuse occurs at a 1,500% higher rate than the national average (National Victim Center, 1993). A recent report by a national commission of enquiry, carried out by the National Society for the Prevention of Cruelty to Children, called "Childhood Matters" (1996), states that 1 million children are harmed every year in the United Kingdom: four children a week die as a result of neglect or abuse, and at least one child out of every thousand under the age of 4 suffers from severe physical abuse such as fractures, brain haemorrhage, severe internal injuries, or mutilation (Meadow, 1989). The figures for child sexual abuse across Europe show that one in three girls and one in ten boys have been abused through physical contact, usually by males known to the family (Halperin et al., 1996).

Though males are the main perpetrators of violence, they are also twice as likely to be victims of violence as females. Teenage boys are four times as likely to commit suicide than their female counterparts, and this difference increases with age, so that at the age of 85 the suicide rate is 1,350 times higher than for females (Farrell, 1993).

Family violence—what is it?

Gelles, a noted researcher in the field of domestic violence, defines violence as an "act carried out with the intention, or perceived intention, of physically injuring another person" (Gelles, 1978). I find it more useful to expand this definition to include the intention of physically or psychologically injuring another person, since the sexual abuse of children often results in severe long-term emotional consequences for the victims but does not necessarily involve physical injury.

The essential ingredient in domestic violence is fear—fear for the victim's safety or fear for the safety of other family members. This is partly why family violence remains such a secret, but it is not the only reason. Victims of family violence live perpetually in the shadow of an all-pervading terror. They may have learnt to cope, as we all do, by cutting themselves off from the source of their pain using the defence mechanisms that keep us going in the face of helplessness and fear. But their terror is usually right there, seeping through their defences. The terror of a child whose family was nearly beaten to death by her military father is brought back to life when as an adult she hears the sounds of boots on the pavement, the screams of her neighbours, or the voice of a male authority figure. What this patient and countless others with similar stories of terror are suffering from is a form of post-traumatic stress disorder originating in childhood abuse. Like the Vietnam veteran who, on hearing a car backfire in the street, is taken physically and mentally back to the battlefront, these patients suffer from the same condition—albeit modified by the process of child development. Though apparently adult in most of their activities, these individuals have remained in part frozen in the terrifying experiences of their childhood. When it comes to re-experiencing anything that takes them back to their past terrifying relationships, they can flip back into their childhood states of total helplessness, dependence, and terror. Even their thinking can return to that of a child who knows s/he cannot survive.

Corporal punishment and the perpetration of violence

Though domestic violence clearly has some disastrous effects in terms of human suffering and social costs, most Western societies advocate the use of physical punishment to bring up our children.

As the old proverb states, *"He that spareth the rod hateth his son but he that loveth him correcteth him betimes"* (Proverbs, XIII, 24). People follow this proverb, though there is little if any advice in the New Testament to support such behaviour and much that contradicts it (Grevin, 1990). In the United Kingdom, as in the United States, 84%–97% of all parents use physical punishment on their children. In a survey of 2,143 American families, Gelles (1978) found that violence well beyond ordinary physical punishment is a widespread phenomenon. It is said to be carried out in the best interests of the victim, but the actual results are disturbing: 46.4% of children between the ages of 3 and 17 have been pushed, grabbed, or shoved, 71% have been slapped or spanked, and about 7.7% (3 to 4 million) have been kicked, bitten, or punched by a parent at some time in their lives. These figures illustrate patterns of regular, normative violence and are low estimates of what really takes place. At the extreme end of the violence spectrum, between 99,000 to 1.8 million children had their parents use a gun or a knife on them.

Straus (1991) points out how physical punishment is a universal phenomenon in the United States involving all Americans either as recipients or as perpetrators. This, he says, is because it is a culturally sanctioned form of abuse central to the "socialization" process:

> Since physical punishment is used by authority figures who tend to be loved or respected and since it is almost always used for a morally correct end when other methods fail, physical violence teaches that violence can and should be used in similar circumstances. [Straus, 1991, p. 134]

As we shall see, this is important in explaining why individuals commit violence so easily when given permission to do so by a figure in authority.

Male–female inequality: the template for interpersonal violence

Domestic violence has its roots in traditional, cultural, and legal support for male dominance in family life. Violence against women is a right that has been exercised with impunity for centuries. Physical violence against wives was seen as necessary for the "well-being" of women. British common law embraced, but limited, the husband's authority to assault wives by adopting, in 1765, the "rule of thumb" which permitted a man to beat his wife with a "rod not thicker than his thumb". In 1821, a judge called Mister Justice Brook declared that "If a man beat an outlaw, a traitor, a pagan, a villain, or his wife, it is dispunishable" (i.e. it is no offence in law). Such a statement is based on the premise that men can rule over, or "have dominion over", those seen as less human, which, to paraphrase the judge, includes criminals, delinquents, non-Christians, and women. The stage is set for the dehumanization of the "other", and this, as will become clearer later on, is a basic cognitive requirement for the propagation of violence in society. As long as those who govern our societies want to retain their power over others, they need to convince those they govern that some people are inferior and less human than themselves. This gives legitimacy to the use and abuse of certain members of society, starting with women. Sexual inequality is still an intrinsic part of the structure of society, so that the dehumanization of the "other" is still a fundamental part of male–female interaction. Even though men appear to have the upper hand, on the whole both men and women suffer in the process. Psychologically, a boy has to get rid of his identification with his first love—his mother. To help him achieve this, the dangerous feminine qualities must be devalued, and women must be seen as potentially bad and worthless. In other words, women must be dehumanized. This can result in men being less able to empathize with others and a turning towards sex and sadism in order to boost their masculinity (Stoller, 1975). In male-dominated societies, women learn to play the part required of them in order to preserve the male's sense of masculinity: as a result, they deny their own needs and are more likely to turn their anger against themselves and their children. Women tend to be the victims and men the offenders (Herman, 1986).

As a result of this culturally sanctioned developmental process in the United States, 21% to 34% of women can expect to be assaulted by a male they know intimately and over 50% can expect to be violently treated by their spouse (National Victim Center, 1993).

One study in the United States showed that 25–30% of men interviewed in college said they would attempt rape if they could get away with it (Malamuth, 1981). Many men perceive women as objects of potential abuse—a developmental outcome that is encouraged by the community in which they live. This is shown quite clearly when Malamuth exposed the same college students to pornographic, sexually violent images of women enjoying being raped, and up to 57% of those males indicated some likelihood that they would commit a rape if they knew they would not be caught.

One of the most visible manifestations of the need for men to dehumanize women is the pornography industry. In 1984, $750 million dollars' worth of pornographic material was sold to 52 million men (Russell, 1993). The representation of sexual violence is very much part of this industry. In the first public hearing on pornography, which was carried out in the United States in 1983, pornography was defined by the lawyer Catherine MacKinnon as being specifically related to the subordination of women.

We define pornography as the graphic, sexually explicit subordination of women through pictures or words, that also includes women dehumanized as sexual objects, things or commodities, enjoying pain or humiliation or rape, being tied up, cut up, mutilated, bruised or physically hurt, in postures of sexual submission or servility or display, reduced to body parts, penetrated by objects or animals, or presented in scenarios of degradation, injury, torture, shown as filthy or inferior, bleeding, bruised, or hurt in a context that makes these conditions sexual. . . . We also propose that the use of men, children or transsexuals in the place of women is pornography. [Everywoman, 1988, p. 2]

The Bill in connection with which these hearings were held was the first attempt to allow those who are represented by pornography as victims to challenge those who profit financially from such representations. It was opposed in the United States largely on the grounds of the First Amendment, which guarantees freedom of speech (Everywoman, 1988). But with the sanctioning of male and female inequality and the legitimization of violence, the template is laid down for further acts of dehumanization towards other "lesser" human beings, such as children, blacks, Jews.

What do these experiences of family and social violence do to the human individual? By many they are seen as a fundamental part of human nature, a phenomenon to be kept under control but not eliminated. But recent research shows that we are in fact dealing with the damaging effects of a cultural and political system that does not take into consideration the psychological and physiological needs of its individuals. What are these?

The importance of attachment behaviour in our understanding of violence

Bowlby (1988) maintained that human infants are preprogrammed to develop in a socially cooperative way. Whether they do or do not finally develop in this direction is largely dependent on how they are treated. Bowlby (1969, 1973, 1980) and his colleagues in the United States have made us aware of the attachment behavioural system we share with other primates. It is a hitherto unrecognized and yet fundamental motivational system in the life and development of human beings, as important as the drive for sex or food. Whilst there is clearly no space here to present the vast literature in this field, which has been reviewed elsewhere (Zulueta, 1993), I will attempt to provide a simplified view of the most important findings in terms of our interest in human violence.

In his study of post-war infants who had been separated from their parents, Bowlby discovered just how severely infants were affected by the loss of their mother. He turned his attention to the studies carried out by Harlow (1974) on rhesus monkeys. In his classic dual mother-surrogate studies, Harlow measured the relative importance of bodily contact as opposed to the satisfaction of nutritional needs by separating infant rhesus monkeys from their mothers and comparing their behaviour when the mother was replaced either with a surrogate soft cloth mother or a surrogate wire mother. Even though the latter had a nursing bottle attached to it, Harlow was able to show that "contact comfort" was the primary factor in the formation of mother–infant affectional bonds. Bolstered by these findings, Bowlby was able to postulate his theory of attachment, in which he suggests that attachment behaviour is an integral part of human nature and one we share with many other species. For Bowlby, the biological function of attachment is to ensure care and protection for the young. It is because of this behavioural system that the human infant selects a primary attachment figure whose whereabouts require constant monitoring. The developing infant remains in close proximity to the caregiver, and, with time, secondary attachment figures also become more important. The attachment system in the infant is activated either by internal cues, such as an illness and discomfort, or by external threats, both of which drive the child to seek protection from the caregiver. If the latter is not available, the infant will protest before showing despair and finally becoming detached. At this point these infants will no longer respond to the return of their mother and might even appear to snub her. As we shall see later, this response is important in our understanding of some kinds of violent behaviour.

Further research with primates reveals how severe are the effects of damage to the attachment system. Harlow was the first to look at the effects of maternal deprivation on rhesus monkeys (Harlow & Mears, 1979). He found that separating newborn infants from their mothers immediately following birth produced gross behavioural abnormalities in these infants. The severity of these abnormalities depended on the amount of time they had been kept in social isolation, which varied from 3 to 12 months. These monkeys were then kept in partial isolation for up to 3 years. At the end of this period, Harlow and Mears reported that:

> practically the only social behaviours that seemed to have matured were fear and aggression, and the animals showed these inappropriately and often explosively. Six-month iso- lates aggressed against infants—an act no normal monkey would consider—but before, during and after the aggres- sive acts, they were frozen with fear even though the infants they faced were only half their size. [Harlow & Mears, 1979, p. 288]

If these previously isolated females, who were unable to have sexual relations, were artificially impregnated, they became grossly inadequate mothers, as Harlow and Mears describe so vividly:

> Very soon we discovered we had created a new animal— the monkey motherless mother. These monkey mothers that had never experienced love of any kind were devoid of love for their infants, a lack of feeling unfortunately shared by all too many human counterparts. . . . Most of the monkey motherless mothers ignored their infants but other mother- less mothers abused their babies by crushing the infants face to the floor, chewing off the infants feet and fingers and, in one case, by putting the infant's head in her mouth and crushing it like an eggshell. Not even in our most devi- ous dreams could we have designed a surrogate as evil as these real monkey mothers. [Harlow & Mears, 1979, p. 289]

These findings relating to maternal deprivation are seen to be the result of damage to the behavioural organization underlying the specific set of social behaviours that mediate social attachments. Kraemer (1985), going on to review the neurophysiological effects of isolation in primates, concludes that deprivation of early social experience may produce changes in the central nervous system's neurochemical processes, which results in altered behaviour. Further research on primate separation studies led scientists to conclude that: (1) attachment behaviour has a psychobiological substrate involving many hormonal systems; (2) it is a form of behaviour partly mediated by opiates. Panksepp and his colleagues (Panksepp, 1984; Panksepp, Siviy, & Normansell, 1985) found that the areas of the brain with the highest levels of opiate receptors are those involved in social bonding, pain perception, and separation distress. Indeed, the distress symptoms produced by separation are similar to those seen in narcotic withdrawal states, and they involve aggressive behaviour. For Panksepp this implies that emotions are at the root of social bonding. Pleasure is the outcome of attachment mediated by endogenous opiates. Separation produces distress and aggression.

The development of these attachment bonds is achieved by a complex process of physical and emotional attunement. Right from the first days of life, the primate infant recognizes its parent, and this allows for the process of attunement to take place between mother and infant. Stern (1985) describes this very well as it unfolds between the human infant and his or her caregiver. If this process of attunement works, it can lead to a state of "affect attunement"—a state of mother–infant interplay where the mother, for example, mirrors her infant's behaviour, either directly or by using a different sensory modality. Thus, for example, she may respond to her child's excited jiggling movement with excited jiggling sounds that match the movement in shape, intensity, and timing; in so doing, she is resonating emotionally with her child and recasting the infant's experience into another form of expression. For Stern, this synchronized behaviour produces a matching of inner states between caregiver and child, an attunement at the level of the affect (Stern, 1985, pp. 140–142).

If this vital process of attunement is disrupted in childhood through deprivation, loss, or any other form of trauma, there are often long-term consequences for the way the individual feels about himself and how he behaves towards others. Although the maintenance of a healthy attachment is critical in childhood, buffering the nervous system and providing an interactional pathway for the development of the self, the need for attachments characterizes humans throughout their life span. Whereas Bowlby believed that attachment behaviour developed purely to provide protection for the young primate, we now know that this process allows young infants' early physiological and hormonal systems to be regulated by their primary caregiver—functions that the infants gradually acquire themselves as they develop (Hofer, 1984).

These important physiological changes are accompanied by parallel emotional and behavioural developments arising from the interaction between mother and infant, which lead to the development of the self and the creation of an inner psychic world of "internal object relations" or "working models". This complex process of psychobiological "attunement" between infant and caregiver is to be replayed throughout the individual's subsequent relationships and is at the heart of the infant's attachment to others. This implies that any disruption of this essential developmental process leads to serious long-term effects, both at a physiological and at a psychological level. Recent research on the effects of chronic stress in children shows that dysregulation of the normal stress response—through chronic abuse, for example—can result in a set of highly dysfunctional and maladaptive brain activities (Perry & Pate, 1994). The brains of these children are exposed to abnormally high levels of neurotransmitters, some of which play a key role in certain phases of neurodevelopment. This can have long-term consequences on the brain and body function of these individuals. Perry believes that there may be a link between childhood trauma and many medical and psychiatric conditions relating to the cardiovascular, the neuroendocrine and the immune systems (Perry, 1994). The damage to the brain that results from child abuse also interferes with normal parenting in the next generation (Teicher, Glod, Surrey, & Swett, 1993).

The biological changes described above are accompanied by profound changes in an individual's sense of self. In a desperate attempt to preserve the vital attachment to its caregiver, the child attempts to cut itself off from memories and experiences that threaten its basic need for the parent. This process of dissociation will result in individuals with a fragmented sense of self or even, in cases of extreme deprivation and abuse, with what was called "multiple personality disorder" and is now referred to as "dissociative identity disorder" (Putnam, 1990).

Thus the trauma of loss, deprivation, and child abuse, whether physical, sexual, or emotional, can all have long-standing effects on our capacity to form relationships, our sense of self, and, in particular, our potential for violent or destructive behaviour (Zulueta, 1993, pp. 64–77). The individual can only exist in relation to the "other". Satisfactory attachments that are essential for our emotional well-being are dependent on our capacity to become attuned to the "other".

Different types of attachment behaviour in relation to the caregiver

As development takes place, infants learn to be alert to the physical and emotional availability of their caregivers. Mothers may be experienced as either rejecting or unpredictable, in which case different strategies for gaining access to the caregiver will be developed. These different responses of the infant to his or her caregivers (mother and/or father) have become the focus of much research in the field of attachment behaviour.

Mary Ainsworth and her colleagues in the United States were the first to show that the way one-year-old infants behaved when reunited with their parent after an enforced separation depended on how sensitively the latter had responded to their needs during infancy (Ainsworth, Blehar, Waters, & Wall, 1978). She assessed this by first observing infants in their home surroundings and then devising a laboratory test, called the Strange Situation Test, which essentially focuses on the way an infant responds to his or her caregiver after a few minutes of separation.

What Ainsworth and her team found using the Strange Situation Test was that 63% of their middle-class infants showed a secure attachment: they usually cried on separation from their mother but responded rapidly to her warm hug on her return. In the nursery or in the home these children were able to form good relations and to tune in to the needs of others—that is, to empathize. The "other" for such an individual is perceived and treated as another human being whose needs can be attended to.

On the other hand, 12% of infants tested were described as showing an "anxious–ambivalent" form of attachment behaviour. These babies were clingy from the beginning and became very distressed when separated from their parent. On their mother's return they showed a great deal of angry ambivalence, both wanting to be close to their parent and, at the same time, arching away from her and resisting their mothers' efforts to soothe them. These insecurely attached infants had been exposed to inconsistent parenting.

Of particular interest to us are the 20–25% of insecurely attached infants who were found to show an "avoidant" response to their mother on her return. In other words, they showed no distress when she left and ignored her on her return, but their rapid heartbeat showed that, despite appearances, their attachment behaviour was in fact strongly activated (Sroufe & Waters, 1977). These infants had either been neglected or rejected, and their "avoidant" behaviour appears to have arisen because they had been placed in an intolerable conflicting situation by their caregiver (Main, 1981). As we know, if threatened in any way, infants will turn to their mother for security. But what if mother becomes threatening or forbids physical contact, as rejecting parents do? In such cases the infants learn to displace their attention elsewhere and thereby "cut themselves off" from feelings of anger and fear so as to be able to remain as close as possible to the parent they totally depend upon. This may be the origin of dissociation as a protective mechanism. The normal child is trying to remain attached to his or her parent but at the same time having to cut off emotionally because of the threat of rejection.

These avoidant children show poor self-esteem and frequent hostility, and as a result their peer interactions are generally negative. These findings were confirmed in a study on 19 pairs of children aged 4 to 5 carried out by Troy and Sroufe (1987). They found that victimization occurred in all the pairs where one or both children were found to show an avoidant attachment response and the other was also insecurely attached, either avoidant or anxious–ambivalent. Children with secure attachment patterns were not observed to be abusers or victims. This study is of particular interest to our study of human violence because it shows two things: secure children do not show needless aggression, whereas avoidant children can become either abusers or victims. This means that they take on board as a behavioural template (or working model) the actual relationship to which they have been subjected and can enact the role either of victim or of victimizer, depending on the context.

In subsequent studies carried out by Professor Main in the United States, another group of infants was identified using the same Strange Situation Test. These infants displayed a strange "disorganized" response to their returning parent, a mixture of "avoidant" and "anxious–ambivalent" behaviour. They behaved in a bizarre and unpredictable manner upon their mother's return. Some suddenly "froze", others withdrew to another side of the room, still others fell to the ground or dived under their mother's chair. This new category of infants appears to have mothers who are very frightening, either because they are abusive to their children or because they have themselves been traumatized and therefore tend to dissociate (Main & Hesse, 1990). Research in this area suggests that when these infants become adults, they may be diagnosed as suffering from borderline personality disorder (Fonagy et al., 1995; Patrick et al., 1994), frequently ending up in psychiatric care if they are female and in prison if they are male. Further evidence is needed to establish whether these same individuals do resort to the more extreme forms of violent behaviour seen in the forensic population. These studies on attachment behaviour patterns have been replicated in many different countries, producing very similar results. Where there are differences, these have been ascribed to cultural differences in upbringing. It is becoming clear that patterns of attachment are self-perpetuating, allowing an individual to preserve a sense of identity, continuity, and predictability.

Familial sources of potential violence

These studies show that avoidant and disorganized infants grow up with a sense of worthlessness that they project onto the world and the people about them. As adults, they are so insecure that they have a desperate need to have some sense of control over others, who can thereby become objects of contempt, abuse, and exploitation.

The avoidant infant learns to cut off his feelings of fear and anger in order to obey and thereby please his parent. The price he pays is that he cannot integrate his feelings of fear and rage that can be triggered off by the pain of another. For these individuals "to do unto others what was done unto them" is a way of being in charge and getting satisfaction or even excitement. When they grow up, they can find their needs for control and revenge fulfilled within the confines and secrecy of the family home or under the orders of an able group leader, who knows how to command and channel their rage to his ends. For these men—and, to a lesser extent, women—the more "legitimate" or socially approved the context of their activity, the more manifest their use of power and control.

The disorganized infants grow up in a state of recurring terror and with a desperate need to feel that they are in control of the world. Without this control, they fear that they will be reduced to the state of helpless terror and pain of their childhood or even to insanity. To understand them better, we will need to look at the research on psychological trauma and what it has to teach us regarding the origins of violence.

Transgenerational transmission

The experience of loss, deprivation, and child abuse, whether physical, sexual, or emotional, can all have long-standing effects on our capacity to form relationships, our sense of self, our potential for violent or destructive behaviour, and even the quality of parenting we provide for our children.

Main and her team developed an Adult Attachment Interview that assesses parental attachment representations (George, Kaplan, & Main, 1985). This semi-structured interview is coded for coherence, for the manner in which individuals describe their childhood relationship with their parents and the way they have dealt with or not dealt with loss and traumatic experiences. One important finding to come out of this research was that it is not the specific events in people's childhood that determine their internal attachment representations, but how much they can look at their early relationships with their caregivers and evaluate them realistically. Those who idealize their parental relationship or who dismiss them as unimportant are the ones who later tend to recreate insecure attachment patterns in their lives. A 75% correspondence exists between parental mental representations of attachment and their infants' attachment security. The authors involved in these studies conclude that the intergenerational transmission of attachment can be considered as an established fact (Van IJzendoorn & Bakermans-Kranenburg, 1997).

These findings are very important, since they provide us with another way of understanding the transgenerational transmission of attachment patterns that may later in life play a part in increasing a person's chance of developing certain conditions, such as post-traumatic stress disorder (PTSD). For example, in a study in the Israeli army on PTSD casualties of the Lebanon war, Solomon, Kotler, and Mikulencer (1988) found that over the three years following the war, the children of Holocaust survivors had greater rates of PTSD than did control subjects whose parents had not been victims of the Nazi genocide. Thus, the transmission of vulnerability to certain psychiatric conditions, which has hitherto been linked to genetic transmission, could also be due to transgenerational transmission via the attachment system.

Psychological trauma as the manifestation of a disrupted attachment system

If psychological trauma is defined as the "sudden uncontrollable disruption of affiliative bonds" (Lindemann, 1944), it is not surprising to find that there is considerable overlap between attachment disorders and psychological trauma, since both result from a disruption of the attachment system.

Post-traumatic stress disorder (PTSD) is a syndrome that recognizes the wounding of the human psyche during states of terrifying helplessness. Whether individuals develop PTSD depends not only on the nature of their experience but also on subjective factors and on the strength of the community attachments that surround them.

This disorder appears as a biphasic response involving, on the one hand, the reliving of traumatic events in some form or other, and, on the other, a sense of numbness and a reduced responsiveness to the outside world as the individual attempts to cut himself off from his source of terror and pain. An understanding of the clinical and biological manifestations of PTSD is important in the treatment of trauma victims, whether they have been traumatized by a single experience or been affected by prolonged and repeated traumatic experiences resulting, for example, from chronic child abuse (Herman, 1992). I will attempt to show how much the psychobiological manifestations of PTSD resemble those seen in infants with disrupted attachments. They appear to involve the same hormonal systems and the psychological defences of dissociation that we first observed in the avoidant infant.

Dissociation and re-enactment

Traumatized people find themselves reliving their traumatic experience mainly through intrusive thoughts such as flashbacks, nightmares, recurrent memories, or—most important to us—the actual re-enactment of the event. In the latter, the subject may play the role of the victim or the victimizer, as we saw with "avoidant" infants earlier on (Troy & Sroufe, 1987). It is this particular consequence of psychological trauma that is an

48   VIOLENCE

important cause of violence and can be at the root of what appears as unprovoked violence occurring many years after the original trauma. In these individuals damage to the attachment system results in such intense terror and accompanying rage that it is often "cut off" or "split off" from consciousness: this means that the individual has no idea why he is doing what he is doing. This phenomenon has been called "traumatic re-enactment". Van der Kolk (1989) provides us with a vivid example from his practice. He describes a patient of his who had fought in Vietnam. One night in 1968, this man had lit a cigarette, which caused the death of his friend by a Viet Cong bullet. From 1969 to 1986, on the exact anniversary of his friend's death, he committed an "armed robbery" by putting a finger in his pocket and carrying out a "hold-up" in order to provoke gunfire from the police. This compulsive and unconscious re-enactment only came to an end when he understood its meaning (p. 391).

This example shows how painful memories can be lost to consciousness because of a failure to integrate traumatic experiences into declarative or conscious memory. They can then be triggered back into action (though not necessarily consciousness) by some external or internal stimulus in order to recreate the pain to which the individual was once subjected, either in himself or in the other, as we see in many parents who abuse their children. When triggered by these kinds of intrusive memories, the traumatized individuals are exposed to states of high arousal that cannot be handled because of an associated inability to modulate such experiences, both psychologically and physiologically. In addition, if they have been subjected to early emotional deprivation, they may have developed less opiate receptors and may therefore need higher levels of opiates to achieve some state of equilibrium and self-soothing. This may result in addictive behaviour, including the compulsive re-exposure to trauma, which in itself releases endogenous opiates (Van der Kolk, 1989, p. 401).

It is becoming clearer that psychological trauma is a psychobiological reaction involving the brain and in particular the amygdala, the hippocampus, and the prefrontal cortex. Van der Kolk (1994) has reviewed some of the changes that take place in the brains of people suffering from chronic PTSD. Bremner and his colleagues (1995) subsequently found that in patients suffering from severe chronic PTSD, the hippocampus is seen to be smaller than normal. In a recent study, Van der Kolk and his team show how, when exposed to a traumatogenic stimulus that brings back memories of the trauma, the brains of patients suffering from PTSD display remarkable changes when examined with the use of brain imaging techniques such as the PET (Positron Emission Tomography) scan (Rauch et al., 1996). Their speech area in the left dominant hemisphere closes down and the right non-dominant hemisphere becomes more active, particularly the occipital area at the back of the brain, which is linked to the brain centres controlling vision. These findings corroborate what we have seen clinically. Traumatized patients often report an inability to speak when they relive traumatic experiences, and many "see things" relating to these experiences (flashbacks).

This research is very important in the study of traumatogenic violence. It is beginning to confirm already existing evidence that psychological trauma does alter the neurophysiology of the brain and even its anatomical appearance (Yehuda & McFarlane, 1995). In a sense, one could say that psychological trauma is a disease with physiological, psychological, and social manifestations. Drug abuse, delinquency, domestic violence and social violence, in all its bloody manifestations can be seen as signs of this disease. It is also transmissible down the generations through the attachment behaviour of parents towards their offspring.

As Bowlby emphasized, human beings are attached to one another through the psychophysiological manifestations of their attachment system, and their self-esteem is linked to this capacity to become attuned to one another through multiple relationships across the lifespan. To ignore this essential aspect of human nature is to do so at our peril, and yet current political, economic, and social institutions do nothing to reduce current levels of violence; on the contrary, they appear to increase the levels of violence in our communities.

The role of political and social institutions
in the propagation of social violence

As a direct result of a violent upbringing that ignores our basic needs for love and care, we create in society a reservoir of people who are capable, in the right circumstances, to carry out very violent acts against others.

The "normal" individual's capacity for violence

Milgram's famous study on *Obedience and Authority* illustrates this normative capacity. In his study, more than 50% of ordinary men were capable of inflicting severe and even life-threatening electric shocks to another individual when told to do so by a scientist in a position of authority (Milgram, 1974). He concludes his study with the following words:

> The kind of character produced in an American democratic society cannot be counted on to insulate its citizens from brutality and inhumane treatment at the direction of a malevolent authority. A substantial proportion of people do what they are told to do, irrespective of the content of the act and without limitations of conscience, so long as they perceive that the command comes from a legitimate authority. [Milgram, 1974, p. 189]

Zimbardo's experiment with students produced similar results in a simulated prison environment (Sabini & Silver, 1982), with highly selected students arbitrarily assigned to either prisoner or warder roles. This study focused on what people can do when they are given legitimate power over another. In fact, the reactions of both groups were so extreme that the experiment had to be stopped after only six days, even though it was meant to go on for two weeks. The fact that the experiment got so out of hand is indicative of the violence that can be unleashed when the setting encourages people to express their destructive feelings. Whereas some "guards" obeyed prison rules and others went out of their way to help their "prisoners", a third of them were extremely hostile and despotic. They invented new forms of degradation and humiliation and appeared to enjoy the power they had.

What these studies suggest to me is that, in conditions where abuse is made legitimate, certain people who have been maltreated in childhood could re-experience their abuse either as victims or as abusers, depending on the power they are given. These assumptions are based on the evidence that the environmental changes and their associated cues many reactivate past traumatic memories (Van der Kolk, 1989). The human potential for destructiveness would be related to the earlier damage inflicted to individual's sense of self-identity and to his or her attachment system. However, in Delgado's (1968) work on aggression in primates, he makes it quite clear that the most essential aspect in the development of violence is the personal reception and processing of environmental information through the various mechanisms of the brain, which, when activated, can induce violent responses. One of the most powerful socio-cultural factors in determining whether human violence is acted out or not is the process of dehumanization.

In Milgram's and Zimbardo's experiments, the authority figure sanctions the dehumanization of the "other"—in one case a student, who, "in the interest of science", must be taught what is "right" and "wrong". For the experimental subjects who experienced corporal punishment in childhood, the authority figure is like the parent who had to be obeyed. But in this case the subject can actually please his authoritarian parent by doing to the student what was done unto him. Didn't he learn that "might is right"? A similar process as that described by Milgram and by Zimbardo takes place in torture chambers across the world, and it is often carried out in the name of "law and order".

Links between legitimate or condoned violence and social violence

Strong links have been found to exist between levels of legitimate or condoned violence and levels of antisocial violence against women. Baron and Straus (1988) show that in a state where: (a) violence is prevalent in the media; (b) violence is used by the government through carrying out the death penalty and allowing corporal punishment in schools; (c) there is high participation in legal violent activities such as shooting, women were eight times more likely to be raped than in a state with lower levels of legitimate violence. This study has the merit of showing a direct link between legitimate violence and antisocial violence. Since the rewards of such systematic violence have always outweighed the costs, particularly for the male sex, there has been little motivation for change. But the levels of social violence and the destructive capacity of our military system are now such a threat to our existence that we must find a new way of raising our children, even though this necessitates change.

The role of the military in maintaining violence

The waging of war is intrinsic to the history of "civilized" society: millions of apparently sensible people have followed their leaders into war and still do so, hence the necessity of having a large reservoir of obedient and potentially violent men to fight our battles. But to achieve this end an "enemy" has to be created, and his dehumanization has to be sanctioned by those in authority. It is no longer possible to deny the importance of the military in the propagation of violence through political and economic pressures as well as through the need to dehumanize or objectify the "other" for the purpose of war and "defence". This is particularly well illustrated by Lifton in the book *Genocidal Mentality*, on the "nuclear bureaucracy" (Lifton & Markusen, 1990).

The social and economic implications of military spending and development in the United States are quite astonishing in terms of the suffering and destruction it produces amongst its own people. It is known that 60 cents of every income tax dollar now goes to the military, while only 2 cents goes to education, for example. The United States spends up to 500 billion dollars per year on its military, which is almost a million dollars per minute (Andreas, 1993). While the federal budget deficit has grown by 400 million dollars per year, the United States has spent more than 9.2 trillion dollars building up its military might between 1948 and 1988. There are noticeable results: cuts in the federal funding for education of 16% over the last decade, cuts of 49% in federal funding for health care, cuts in federal funding for housing of 77% (Andreas, 1993). In the United States, the richest nation in the world, a child dies every 50 minutes of poverty or hunger (Andreas, 1993). In the United Kingdom, 10% of our taxes go to the military, some of it into government research tied to military projects and in promoting arms sales.

The U.S. media are very much involved in backing the American military–industrial complex, convincing people of the need to build up America's military potential, and fighting crime (Andreas, 1993). This entire process involves the dehumanization of the "other", the creation of an "enemy". With the collapse of the Soviet Union, new enemies had to be found. There is now a trend in the U.S. military industry to move into the law-and-order business on the domestic front, a booming part of the "war against crime". By the mid-1990s the United States was spending in excess of $200 billion annually on the crime control industry. At a meeting involving both the army and penal system, the U.S. Secretary of Defence was heard saying, "you won the war abroad, now win the war at home". Hagan concludes his analysis of the American Penal System as follows:

> The new language in the United States is of *efficient management*, with an emergent emphasis on handling large numbers of offenders by classifying them in *subpopulations*, which are identified as specially *dangerous* and in need of *selective incapacitation* through imprisonment. This has resulted not only in an exponential growth in the imprisonment of young *minority* offenders but also in the development of a widened range of coercive sanctions that include boot camps, electronic surveillance and house arrest, high security "campuses" for drug users, and intensive forms of parole and probation. [Hagan, 1994]

There are now nearly two million people in prison and another three and a half million under penal control in the United States on any given day (Miller, 1996). The number of people in custody for part of the year, in any one year, comes to more than 10 million, and they are mainly men (J. Gilligan, 1996). The current policy is to increase spending and incarceration. In California the new "three strikes you're out" policy was backed by the prison guards' association (Christie, 1995). It will cost an additional $5.5 billion in criminal justice expenditures. The same prison guards' association gave millions to the politicians for the expansion of the prison industry (Christie, 1995). It is not clear yet whether or not the new British government will follow a similar policy. Under the conservatives, the British penal system was following the U.S. pattern. Whilst more prisons are being built and more offenders are being punished, very little is being done to prevent crimes of violence either in the home or in society, and even less in prison. Around one million criminals leave every year in a worse state than they went in as a result of being raped by their fellow inmates. As James Gilligan (1996) points out, those outside the prison system will pay the price of their traumatization.

The human damage carried out by the penal system does not stop here. It severely penalizes drug offenders: 60% of prisoners are locked up in the United States for drug offences, whether or not they also have a record of violent crime. Most of these inmates are African–Americans. Even though the U.S. Public Service estimated in 1992 that 76% of illicit drug-users were white, 14% black, and 8% Hispanic, 92% of all drug-possession offenders sentenced to prison were black and Hispanic in New York State and 71% in California. Between 1930 and 1972, 455 people were executed for rape in the United States, 405 of them black (Kaminer, 1995). This racial bias is also present in Canada and in the United Kingdom, though in a less extreme form.

Inequality and poverty, the deadliest source of violence

James Gilligan, director of the Center for the Study of Violence at Harvard Medical School, describes as "structural violence" the increased rates of death and disability suffered by those who occupy the bottom ranks of society, contrasted with the lower death rates and morbidity experienced by the wealthier and those in higher strata of society. Structural violence is far more deadly than violence caused by armed conflict. A world-wide study carried out by Kohler and Alcock (1976) showed that 14 to 18 million people die every year from the effects of poverty, whilst about 100,000 die from armed conflict. Recent research shows a clear relationship between economic policy and increasing inequality in health. The most interesting aspect of this research is that these effects are not linked to levels of poverty but to the degree of inequality. For example, not only has the difference in mortality between the rich and the poor widened, but those excluded from the general prosperity also suffer in many other ways. Young men in this group show in-creased levels of suicide, of crime, of drug misuse, and of vio-lence (Watt, 1996, pp. 26–29).

Conclusions

The seeds of violence are implanted from infancy onwards, to be fostered and used when those in authority require it—even at the cost of violence in our families and in our streets.

Dehumanization is central to the final manifestation of vio-lence, allowing those whose rage and destructiveness is split off to express their feelings on those whom their group, their com-munity, or those in authority have deemed less human than themselves, be they children, women, foreigners, blacks, homo-sexuals, or the poor.

Dehumanization is also essential to the process of social con-trol and to current economic policies, which are manifested in the creation of inequality. The resultant poverty could be seen as another form of dehumanization, and we now know that inequality per se engenders violence.

There is little doubt that there is a huge scientific and politi-cal investment in the notion that violence is both morally evil and an inextricable part of human nature. As James Gilligan (1996) says, so long as we can morally blame the violent and see them as "evil monsters" rather than as damaged human beings, we can punish them. And punishment is a form of violence in its own right—albeit a legally sanctioned one. Both in the home and in society, it allows people to inflict pain in retribution, to dominate and humiliate others in the service of gaining pride and power by giving the "bad and evil" what they deserve. Punishment, however, does nothing to reduce violence—on the contrary, it increases it.

The prevention of violence will therefore require a public health approach that puts the attachment needs of the individual child, woman, and man at the centre of its campaign. The remedy against violence lies within us: humans are all born with the potential and the need to make loving relationships. For this potential to develop, however, it is necessary to change the way people think about themselves and the world they live in. As Einstein said: "We shall require a substantially new way of thinking if mankind is to survive."

CHAPTER THREE

Creating a non-violent environment: keeping sanctuary safe

Joseph F. Foderaro

Introduction

In 1986, Dr Stephen Silver, in his work with Vietnam veterans, used the term "sanctuary trauma" to describe the impact that an inhospitable, unsafe, and disrespectful health care system had on the returning veterans of combat experiences (Silver, 1986). He maintained that for those who had been subjected to traumas, a safe and sane environment was critical to the development and redeployment of constructive intrapsychic and social defences; otherwise, patterns of maladaptation were bound to continue. But what constitutes a safe and sane environment, and what methodology contributes to creating and maintaining such a milieu? The goal of this chapter is to provide a concrete example of a small psychiatric unit struggling to answer these questions with a view to providing suggestions for an approach to any community searching for the means to end violence.

Sanctuary—not just a place

Since 1980, a team of clinicians has been striving to create an environment that would not create sanctuary trauma but would, instead, provide a place within which safe healing from trauma could begin. The *Sanctuary®* Programs, now located in two private psychiatric hospitals in Pennsylvania and New Jersey, are short-term inpatient psychiatric units dedicated to working with adult survivors of abuse, other traumatic experiences, and long-term and severe neglect. *Sanctuary* started off, and remains to this day, an experiment that uses the tools of social psychiatry towards the goal of creating and maintaining a safe and sane therapeutic experience for those whose patterns of life necessitate such a reconstructive experience (Bloom, 1997).

Like many other psychiatric units, *Sanctuary* found itself over a decade ago being hosted by à hospital located in a community that had ambivalent feelings about having such a programme in its midst. Stereotyped assumptions about psychiatric patients abounded, and there was great pressure put upon the programme to be as inconspicuous as possible. Paradoxically, this meant that the unit would have to be, among other things, unlocked. In a rural community that still believed in the fantasy, if not reality, of safe streets, locked doors would have brought even more attention to the unit from community leaders. Therefore, *Sanctuary*, from its inception, presented itself as a programme that would not, and did not, depend on the external security of locked doors to ensure its own—and by extension, the community's—safety. Not that such security was totally absent. Good psychiatric and nursing practices include learning techniques for the pharmacological and physical management of the out-of-control patient. Proper restraint procedures, quiet rooms, and pharmacological restraints are all accepted medical and milieu-management practices. Perhaps most significantly, *Sanctuary* has always emphasized that such interventions should not distract from the inherent assumption of the programme: that the locus of control over violent impulses must develop from within the individual. This contrasts with those programs and units that impose control, sometimes arbitrarily, from externally placed structures. This assumption about the need for control to be developed from within may be the basic distinguishing feature that separates *Sanctuary* from many other clinical programs. There is a notable difference between therapeutic experiences that are supportive and protective in nature and those that assume a truly rehabilitative nature. For the latter to occur, assumptions about personal limitations must be challenged, tested, and allowed to develop, and there has to be compelling community pressure for the violence-prone individual to adopt a different set of values. Although it is unarguable that the administration of *Sanctuary* has, as a primary responsibility, the security of its population to maintain, it is a recurrent theme that this responsibility is shared with all of the participants of the programme.

Sanctuary is, first and foremost, a programme that is voluntarily requested by those who decide to seek entrance. With only very rare exceptions, all participants must be willing to register themselves, and not be mandated by a civil or criminal court system, to be admitted to the programme. This means, therefore, that there is a certain selectivity to the patient sample found in the programme. This selectivity is not necessarily in terms of level of dangerousness, but certainly in terms of motivation to change. In its history, *Sanctuary* has included as participants in its programmes those who have attempted suicide by self-inflicted shotgun blast, overdosing to the point of coma, self-inflicted lacerations resulting in unconsciousness due to blood loss, and sexual acting-out with at-risk populations without any "protection". These represent only a small sampling of behaviours nearly guaranteed, eventually, to ensure self-annihilation. Such violence is not, of course, only directed towards the self. Individuals who have served "hard time" for murder or for manslaughter (of a child), those who have served or are about to serve a jail sentence for paedophilic activities, some who have attempted to poison, suffocate, or otherwise eliminate their parents, and others who have been the perpetrators of violence or abuse themselves have also participated in the *Sanctuary* programme. Those who criticize *Sanctuary* for its selectiveness cannot do so based solely on clinical indicators. What is required of its participants, however, is a commitment to *Sanctuary* that the

programme, its physical space, and those enrolled in the programme will be honoured and respected as a violence-free zone.

Trauma-based treatment, as offered by *Sanctuary*, is com-
prised of a number of specific modalities of individual and
group therapies, all intended to help the individual and community address issues of violence and recovery. There are clear
proscriptions against any form of physical or verbal violence
while an individual is residing in the unit. All clinical interventions with the client are intended to allow for exploration of
the themes of abuse while, at the same time, encouraging individuals to learn to set appropriate boundaries around such
expressions so that they do not, in and of themselves, become
provocative and damaging in their own right. All therapies
found in *Sanctuary*, including the evocative therapies of psy-
chodrama, movement therapy, and art therapy, are titrated in
their intensity so that the participants are able to remain focused and in control of the therapy and expressive process, as
otherwise such therapies can unintentionally lead to re-enactments of graphic portrayals of past traumas that do little to
leave the group participants with a sense of mastery and control
or safety.

One does not have to look far to find people who have been
seriously impacted by the forces of violence. Directly or indirectly, our entire world is steeped in a culture of violence and
exploitation. Aggression, when it does not actually destroy its
victim, all too often serves to embolden the victim to pass it on,
like a cold virus, to some other unsuspecting or vulnerable soul.
This is why violence has been, and remains, a public health
menace. There are too many people in the world who have been
seriously hurt for us to ignore them. They are prepared to ex-
pend the energy that violence begets in order to pass it on to
others in a short-cut attempt to empower the self. When not
passed on to others, this violence frequently becomes self-di-
rected and manifests itself as one of many forms of self-destructiveness. *Sanctuary* attempts to provide an alternative to the
maintenance of a status quo in which violence and aggression is
only recycled.

The inherent lure of violence is often seen in the context of
doing therapy on the unit. In the same way that horrific acci-

dent scenes create a logjam of "rubberneckers" who often ex-
pose themselves to greater danger in order to catch a glimpse of
the accident, the therapeutic arena is often the scene of clinicians and patients alike who are intrigued, if not outright en-
tranced, by the specific details of past traumas and abuses.
Frequently patients will request to do specific "work" about
this material, and if this is done without proper safeguards of
affect monitoring, such "work" often leads to regressive behaviour by participants and observers alike. Perhaps even more
importantly, if patients are unable to learn the skills of affect
modulation in the context of therapy, it is unlikely that such
skills will be utilized after or in-between therapies, when the
actual implementation of learned therapeutic skills can be prac-
tised. Often a patient or their therapist will feel that the patient
has done "a lot of work" in an individual or group session. But
if this work is not accompanied by affect modulation, insight,
and closure, then there will often be a negative carry-over effect
upon the rest of the client population after the "working day" is
over, when the unit management becomes the primary responsibility of nursing staff alone. It is easy to mistake emotional
expression occurring in a dissociated state for important therapeutic work. Abreaction is not sufficient, nor does it guarantee
improvement unless it is accompanied by integration with affect, thought, and judgement.

Those who participate in the *Sanctuary* programme often
identify themselves as being among the most thoughtful and
considerate individuals to be found. Although they readily admit that they rarely are considerate or respectful to themselves,
they often emphasize that "I would never hurt anyone else". In
fact, these individuals rarely reflect upon the consequences that
self-abusive destructiveness—or even tempestuous acting-out
behaviours—can have on the therapeutic milieu. The nature
and impact of such behaviour is often minimized and distorted
through the self-absorbed and, at times, narcissistically biased
filters of rationalization and denial. It is amazing how a person
can proclaim their safety to others even as their self-inflicted
wounds are being sutured or their stomachs pumped. People
tend to maintain a marked distinction between violence against
self and violence against others. In fact, as research demon-

strates and patients often corroborate, self-harming behaviour and suicidal ideation are often experienced as being more soothing in nature than overtly threatening and therefore are usually not appreciated for being of the violent nature that they, in fact, are. First and foremost, *Sanctuary* emphasizes that in order for a constructive and restorative experience to be possible, violence in any form must be renounced as an acceptable coping skill. This is an orientation that is made early on and often in the treatment experience and sets the stage for further interventions that may later question an individual's motivation for change.

A frequently told parable that illustrates this point of violence and commitment to change is the story of Hernan de Cortes and his arrival in the New World with a boatload of conquistadors. Upon landing in South America after a frighteningly long and dangerous trip, Cortes had his boats burnt down to the waterline. Needless to say, some explanation was demanded of him for this apparently insane and self-defeating behaviour, and when given the opportunity to describe his reasons for having the boats burned, he replied to his men: "Now you have no choice but to go forward." This act ensured that there would be minimal risk of mutiny and retreat in the face of the very real dangers of conquering new peoples for fame and fortune. Escape is always an attractive alternative for those faced with exceptionally difficult and dangerous tasks, and there is little that any therapist can offer to a trauma survivor that compares to the allure of eternal peace when the therapeutic process encounters rough times. Escape through self-destruction is a powerful temptation, and when it is compared to the responsibilities that a person must maintain in order to remain alive and well it is not surprising that many survivors find it easier to "give up" and die.

No therapist can assure the patient that future traumas will never occur and that there will be no heartbreaks or financial disasters. Therefore, with suicide always in the background as a viable option to the patient, therapeutic discussions often focus on safety issues rather than on the more reconstructive issues of grief, reconciliation (with oneself and others), and how to use emancipation from trauma as a way of moving on with one's life. Those who travel to *Sanctuary* and take advantage of the programme are reminded that, in spite of the distance travelled and the money spent, therapy in *Sanctuary* does not even begin until one is able to harness the impulse to escape from violence through the further violation of self or others.

In the past few years there has been a significant reduction in the time available to provide inpatient services to those in need, and insight is a goal that is increasingly more difficult to achieve. Interventions must be clear, concise, and relatively unambiguous. Language must be relatively free from the "psychobabble" for which the field of psychiatry is noted. When addressing those with self-harming or aggressive impulses or histories, two words are frequently used to describe the roles of those who live either in a state of fear by threatening others: "terrorist" and "hostage". These words represent the extreme sides of the same violent, exploitative, and vulnerable relationship—exactly the type of relationship from which most traumatic abuse survivors come. Both words describe the early dynamics of a childhood steeped in abuse and violence. The unpredictable and dangerous authority of an abusive parent, exerting control over a vulnerable and terrified child, is quite similar to the process in which a violence-prone individual uses the threat of destruction of self or others if their immediate needs are not met. The terror of a hostage is a familiar concept easily appreciated by most abuse survivors. When the constant threat of suicide is discussed in the same context as the terror inflicted upon a child by an abusive or dangerous authority, there is usually an immediate recognition that the line between perpetrator and victim is finer than originally thought. It is often more difficult for the chronically suicidal or self-destructive person to realize that their violent behaviour represents the empowerment of an individual who uses terror to control. Suicidal and self-destructive threats represent the power of life and death. Individuals who abuse such power if and when they deem it appropriate show as little regard for their victim as their abuser had originally shown for them. In *Sanctuary*, power is described in graphic terms such as this. The constructs of power and control are often raised in therapy, and the client is encouraged to exercise both. However, the client is also encouraged to exercise a moral choice over how this power and control is to be exercised. Will it necessitate, as part of its expression, a damaging of self or another, or can this power be used to create constructive change? Will the patient identify with the perpetrator and carry on the violence, or will he or she choose for the good? This question is often asked of *Sanctuary* patients, who are reminded that any person powerful enough to take a life is equally powerful enough to save a life. Historically, clinicians were discouraged from wandering into areas of morality. In our work with abuse survivors, no such apparent indifference or avoidance is possible.

If in this discussion the *Sanctuary* programme seems to insist upon strict adherence to a code of non-violence and to exercise a dogmatic and judgemental approach to behaviours involving violation of these tenets, so be it. Too frequently, *Sanctuary* patients have described backgrounds in which no clear messages or boundaries had been established or maintained. Instead, messages within the family were filled with ambiguity and opportunity for misinterpretation. In a short-term, closely managed in-patient setting, messages must be clear and boundaries must be defined. Otherwise, there are too many opportunities for the type of manipulation and limit-testing frequently found in more traditional in-patient units. When it comes to matters of life and death and matters of respect for self and others, staff members are strongly encouraged to refrain from hiding behind a mask of therapeutic neutrality. Although the staff readily acknowledges that all *Sanctuary* patients do, indeed, have the power of life and death over themselves and others, it does not mean that the individual has the right to exercise this power in destructive ways. Having the power to inflict havoc upon self or others is a reality that is readily conceded. This is one of the ways in which an individual's sense of power is readily acknowledged. However, once the presence of this power has been recognized, the discussion turns to whether or not a person has the right to exercise this power in destructive ways. A survivor of trauma who insists upon the right to do so indirectly acknowledges that the perpetrator also had a right to do what he or she did, and this realization creates a cognitive dissonance that allows for further exploration of alternatives to acting-out behaviour. Too often, abuse survivors had been tortured and tormented by those who had the power to do so. An important part of the recovery process is to remind survivors that having the power to abuse and neglect is not to be equated with assuming the right to do so, and this is where the element of choice is introduced into the therapeutic process. It is this decision to exercise choice about whether to harm or to help that is the fundamental beginning of the therapeutic process. It is this decision that ultimately determines whether a survivor's life will be an improvement over a traumatic past or continue to be a re-enactment of it. A lifetime of being haunted by memories of abuse and trauma can leave anyone feeling emasculated, vulnerable, angry, and out of control. Chronic passivity and an identity as a victim are major impediments when initiating a therapeutic challenge. With little time allowed for treatment due to issues of financial reimbursement, the proper utilization of clinical resources and therapeutic dilemmas must be quickly and clearly articulated if the treatment experience is to be anything more than an exercise in containment. As a result, a major shift in the client's personal schema is pursued. The hope is that if an individual can truly perceive the intrinsic violent nature of self-annihilation, there can be a significant challenge to the self-perception of impotency and vulnerability. When such a shift occurs, there is then hope that power can be sought out and used in other less destructive ways.

Thus far, it would appear that the primary mode of intervention in the cycle of violence is a quasi-philosophical or theoretical challenge to a survivor's sense of right and wrong. This is, indeed, a vital and inescapable part of the therapeutic process, but it is not the only intervention offered. All the words available to a therapist doing "talking therapy" seem insufficient to serve as a counterbalance to a lifetime of abuse, violence, pain, and intimidation of self or others. Equally important in *Sanctuary* is the availability of a clearly defined strategy of interventions to be used when the unit is subjected to the consequences of violent action. From the onset of the treatment process, participants in the programme are invited, instructed, and expected to participate fully and collectively in the task of keeping *Sanctuary* safe. Although many newly admitted patients expect *Sanctuary* to be something that is being offered to them upon admission, patients are counselled that an admission to *Sanctuary* is, more accurately, an opportunity to learn how to create *Sanctuary* for oneself and others. In this manner, the safety that is alluded to in the *Sanctuary* name becomes a goal that is pursued, rather than a gift that is offered. The patient, therefore, becomes an active part of the *Sanctuary* process, instead of a passive recipient of an environmental condition. The avoidance of the passive role is critical in any therapeutic interaction between staff and patients, or amongst patients themselves. A reenactment of a violent past is nearly inevitable if the patient maintains a passive role of receptivity, instead of assuming an active participant role.

Although the term "patient" has thus far been used in describing the *Sanctuary* programme, this is used in deference to *Sanctuary*'s present location at a psychiatric hospital rather than to any underlying assumption about trauma survivors. In practice, participants in the programme are quickly discouraged from using, and hopefully believing that they are, indeed, the "patient". As a "patient", there is an assumed passivity that directly contradicts the active model that the programme espouses. The patient status also indirectly communicates the right of participation in the programme even if one chooses not to adhere to safe behaviours. Historically, most participants in the programme have come from backgrounds in which there was direct or tacit acceptance of violent or destructive behaviours. Regardless of the activity or consequences upon children, families, or others, this background suggests that complacency or denial were accepted coping strategies to be used when faced with such activity. Such norms must be countered with an equally strong and consistent message that destructive behaviours are, indeed, a threat to ALL *Sanctuary* residents and staff, and as such they cannot be accepted, condoned, nor ignored. Although this is rather easy to articulate, it is, in fact, difficult fairly and constructively to instruct, and it cannot be arbitrarily or unfairly enforced.

Norma B

Norma B was an obese, physically intimidating female who was given to angry, verbally aggressive outbursts when feeling overwhelmed by uncomfortable affect or when she felt she was being treated unfairly. When sad, she would often begin wailing in loud and plaintive ways, and when angry, her wailing would be interspersed with equally loud and aggressive threats and complaints.

After a few days of such behaviour, it was apparent that the community was becoming increasingly intimidated by her. Group leaders noticed less participation by other patients in the group therapy sessions when Norma participated. She was beginning to sense the isolating effects of an entire patient community engaged in avoidant behaviours. Although staff members took on an active role of identifying such behaviours and their consequences, this did not prevent Norma from throwing a tray of food in the general direction of a nurse when this nurse was attempting to engage in some dialogue with her. Immediately sensing that an important rule had been violated, Norma attempted to minimize this by emphasizing that this should not be construed as a violent act, for "I would have thrown it right at her if I wanted to hurt someone".

At this point, Norma was instructed to engage in a "staffing". This term is used to describe a meeting of patient and instrumental staff members, during which an individual's progress is discussed and problem areas are identified and openly discussed. A staffing is an incredibly effective treatment strategy, for it accomplishes much at time. First and foremost, it provides for an opportunity for all participants in the therapy process to discuss the issues at the same time, thus reducing potential problems with miscommunication or splitting. Perhaps equally important is the message that staff is involved and caring enough to participate in such a discussion and eager to give the patient the "attention" they are seeking. Although most patients initially fear such an encounter, believing that it will be a group attack upon them, this fear is quickly dispelled if the staff members strive to remain focused on constructive alternatives to maintaining the same destructive or ineffective patterns. Many patients leave such a meeting with a sense that, perhaps for the first time, they are being watched over and cared about in ways that do not recreate the same shaming and neglecting patterns of their families of origins. Staffings are often considered an important adjunct to the overall therapy experience.

In Norma's case, however, a staffing proved to be ineffective as a way to influence a constructive change, and when she became more verbally threatening again, she was advised that she would have to be transferred to another, more secure unit. Although Norma strenuously opposed such a transfer, maintaining that such action was unwarranted since no one was injured, she did allow for this transfer when the detrimental impact that such behaviour was having upon the community was emphasized. It was important to impress on Norma that this action was being taken as a safeguard to protect others from her aggressive nature and was not merely punitive in nature. Norma was advised that when trauma-work seems to evoke an escalation of violence, then instead of doing more work, a different type of work is required. Norma was also told that if she showed an improved ability to provide proper containment of her affect in ways that allowed for ventilation without intimidation, readmission to the *Sanctuary* programme would be considered.

When the decision to transfer was then put into action, Norma reluctantly complied with the plan. Of course, Norma did not really wish to be excluded from the programme. But she was reminded that in *Sanctuary*, the integrity of the overall community had to be maintained, and that if that conflicted with the specific requirements of any particular patient, then the community's needs would be addressed first. Norma, in a role as "woman–child", was thus reminded that she would not be able to hold hostage an entire community of patients and staff, and that it was her responsibility to recognize that this was the impact of her behaviour.

The unit to which Norma was transferred had its own thera-peutic milieu, although it was significantly different from *Sanctuary* in that it was locked and was lacking in any "trauma-based" work. Norma was also reminded that this transfer represented a failure on the part of *Sanctuary* to exert a strong enough positive influence upon her regarding her impulsive and disruptive behaviours. She was told that if she wished to continue working with a clinician from *Sanctuary* while on another unit, this would be arranged.

After she "cooled off", Norma chose to maintain a connec-tion with *Sanctuary*, and staff members continued to meet with her on the other unit. Over the next few days, she was encouraged to reflect, write in her journal, and discuss those ways in which she might be able to negotiate a re-entry into the community, should she be able to present herself in a more controlled way. After a few days of serious reflection and journaling, Norma signalled her readiness to re-enter *Sanctuary*. Although promising to be "good" if allowed to return, Norma was reminded that it was not a matter of being "good" but, rather, one of being effective in promul-gating *Sanctuary* values regarding respect and safety. This was an important distinction to be emphasized, for a prom-ise to be "good" maintained Norma in the role of a child who had to behave for the powerful parent figure (i.e. staff), whereas her agreement to be safe and respectful would sug-gest more the behaviour of an empowered adult. When this distinction appeared to be appreciated by the patient, Norma was told that she might be ready to address the en-tire community to negotiate a re-entry into it. Norma thus had to face directly those individuals who were impacted by her past behaviours—client and staff alike. The context for this would be arranged during the usual morning commu-nity meeting, and Norma was coached on ways of accepting and acknowledging feedback from the community.

For this patient, this event proved to be even more anxiety-provoking than the original events surrounding her transfer from *Sanctuary*, and the prospects of this exposure and consequent vulnerability tapped into other issues of vulnerability which her weight and bluster effectively masked. It was not an easy meeting for Norma, and it required the active participation of staff to help reassure all parties that the process of reconstructing a safe relationship was essential not only for Norma's sake, but for all members of the community. In this fashion, it became a community task to re-establish the importance of safety and respect as vital elements in the *Sanctuary* programme. Norma was able to manage a successful re-entry into the programme and later became a powerful ally and advocate for the milieu when unrelated events precipitated additional crises. Years later, she has successfully reintegrated into post-graduate studies, remains in outpatient therapy, and has not required rehospitalization for many years.

Unsafe behaviour does not always take its form in throwing things at walls, at others, or in the form of self-injurious actions. Continued disrespect and transgressions of important rules can also have a profound and corrosive impact on a community's sense of security.

Anita C

Anita C, a young adult woman, had an extensive history of hospitalizations and self-destructive behaviours. Carrying a diagnosis of Dissociative Identity Disorder, she customarily explained her resistance to change as "I don't know how to stop it" or "I don't remember doing that". During two different admissions, years apart, she demonstrated behaviour that was potentially very dangerous to her physical well-being and to overall community integrity. During her first admission, she absconded from the hospital and was found in the parking lot, leaning against the brick wall of the hospital. She began by slowly and lightly hitting the back of her head against the wall and gradually continued to hit her head ever harder against the brick. All efforts to engage in conversation were met with closed eyes and continued head-banging, and it was clear that the next intervention would have to be of a physical nature. The obvious response was to call for assistance to restrain her physically and forcefully from this behaviour. This was, indeed, what was contemplated, but before this step was taken, the clinician lightly cradled the back of her head with his hand, imposing his hand between the wall and her head. This patient was reminded that there was now another body part to be considered in addition to her own head as she continued to bang, and she immediately de-escalated the intensity of banging to just a slight tapping. As if to get the last word in, she tapped a few more times and then stopped entirely. She was thanked for her consideration of the clinician's health, strongly encouraged to exercise a similarly safe restraint when it came to her own health, and escorted back to the unit.

Although Anita continued to test some limits as well as the strength of the walls with episodic periods of head-banging, she did no harm to either wall or head for the rest of this stay.

An important message in this vignette is the very real presence and awareness of concern for others even when a patient is deeply entrenched in a dissociatively induced pattern of self-damaging behaviour.

During a later stay in *Sanctuary*, Anita's behaviour was especially disruptive to the smooth functioning of the unit because it involved the continual testing of the open-door policy. Because there was great pressure on *Sanctuary* to curtail such behaviour by closing and locking its doors, staff felt extra pressure to make an effective and timely intervention. Anita continued to abscond from the unit, even when put on visual precautions within sight of staff. At times she would sneak off when she thought she was noticed; at other times she would just run off the unit as quickly as possible. Each time she left the unit, she would not go very far; it was clear that for Anita, the thrill was in the chase rather than in the prospect of escape. Each time she left the unit, she blatantly advertised the impotency of staff to curtail her disruptive and destructive behaviour. For Anita, this was a re-enactment of her father's inability to stop a neighbour from sexually abusing his daughter, even when there was a wealth of clinical signs that something terrible was happening.

Eventually, more active intervention was required, since such a blatant disregard for unit rule was having a profoundly negative impact on clients and staff alike. It seemed that the only effective means of intervention would be to lock the doors of the unit, thus punishing the entire community, or to transfer Anita to a more secure unit or hospital.

Before this was done, however, an intervention was made just prior to another escape. This intervention turned out to be quite effective and was remarkably simple in its strategy. Anita was noticed by staff to be pacing at an escalating speed, becoming increasingly agitated, and looking longingly at the open space beyond the doors of the unit. It was obvious that another escape was imminent. Just before this occurred, a staff member approached Anita and invited her to the very edge of the threshold, just to the point where *Sanctuary* ended and the open hall began. Anita was asked to look closely at the invisible line on the floor that separated the outside world from *Sanctuary*. She was told that although this line was invisible, it was, in fact, the most important part of the *Sanctuary* programme. It was that threshold between *Sanctuary* and the world that made the space inside the unit special, and that this boundary was as important to *Sanctuary* as her own flesh, skin, and blood should have been vital and safe for her as a child. Anita was reminded that the reason she was in *Sanctuary* in the first place was due to the flagrant disregard and disrespect that her perpetrators had shown towards her own body as a child. They exhibited no regard at all for the barrier of her skin, flesh, or body, and crossed and entered these boundaries at will. The staff member acknowledged that when Anita's boundaries were first abused and disregarded, there may have been no effective way for anyone to protect her physical, emotional, and spiritual self from unlawful and immoral incursions, and for that lack of intervention she still suffered.

This summarization of Anita's past earned the staff member her undivided attention, at which time the following point was made. Anita was reminded that her history of having her physical boundaries continually disregarded and violated was, indeed, unfortunate. However, this did not, in any way, warrant her continued active disregard and disrespect for boundaries defined by *Sanctuary* to be necessary to protect all within its confines. She was reminded that *Sanctuary* had to work very hard to maintain its open-door policy; current trends in hospital-based psychiatry tend to accept the premise that locked doors are a minimum requirement for good and safe treatment. Anita was reminded that each time she violated the boundaries defined by the threshold of the open door, she was violating accepted and agreed-upon boundaries of safety as codified by community mores. Therefore, each and every time she left the unit, she was actually assaulting the physical boundaries of *Sanctuary*, as she herself had been assaulted as a child. This was a way of endangering the entire community, and, in fact, was not an exaggeration at all. As Anita's behaviour escalated, and staff were slow to respond in ways that constructively harnessed this energy, other members of the community began to complain about the patient. Many suggested that she be expelled from the community, and a significant minority, instead of complaining, actually began to demonstrate an escalation in their own maladaptive behaviours. This created an additional risk of other abscondments or even more dangerous behaviours. Anita was given the choice, after some discussion, of either helping to keep *Sanctuary* safe by curbing her impulses to run or of continuing to be, in a sense, a perpetrator against community mores. This paradigm was met with a startled, guilty, and remorseful response, followed by a slow return to her room. Later that day, without prompting by staff, Anita apologized to the community. In a few subsequent admissions over a protracted period of time, Anita never again attempted to leave the unit.

Externalized aggression is managed in the same way. Community proscriptions against violence are explicitly reviewed in a variety of formats. Community meetings, group therapy, and individual therapy all provide forums in which the non-violent theme of recovery from traumatic events is constantly emphasized. Having a unit that treats both men and women victims of violence has made maintenance of a safe unit more interesting, albeit more difficult. There is an assumption, based as much on gender bias as on fact, that the unit is inherently more dangerous if men are allowed to be part of the programme. Actually, in an 18-year history of in-patient psychiatric management, there has yet to be a physical confrontation (either physical or sexual) between patients on the unit. Two staff members have been hit (both incidents involved female patients and staff), and neither incident required more of a response than an incident report. On both occasions, however, swift intervention was effected. In the first event, a request was made of the patient to meet with staff, and she was reminded of community proscriptions of violence and the need for everyone to participate in the process of keeping *Sanctuary* safe. A failure to do so would be interpreted as a failure to agree to a basic treatment contract with the programme. This particular patient accepted responsibility for her behaviour, apologized to staff and community alike, and completed her hospital stay with no further acting-out behaviour. The second incident involved a young woman who was drug-dependent and who was unwilling to give any type of assurance that such behaviour would not reoccur. She reminded all that "no one was safe should they get in (her) face". She was unmotivated for treatment and seemed to be using the programme to fulfil a need for anti-anxiety and pain-reducing medication. Presenting no clear and present danger to self or others (the physical assault was more of a push than a strike), the patient was administratively discharged back into the community. During the following months she made repeated attempts to secure a readmission to *Sanctuary*. Each time, she and her outpatient therapist were reminded of the requirement that she adhere to a non-violent and sober theme during her recovery. Although this particular patient made repeated assurances about her ability to remain safe in *Sanctuary*, she demonstrated no commitment at all to establishing a sobriety plan. She was advised that the theme of safety, once violated, needs to be re-established by way of behavioural responses; verbal assurances are insufficient to re-establish trust. She was advised that to secure readmission, a period of 90 days of sobriety would have to be maintained, either as an outpatient or as a participant in a chemical dependency programme. This prerequisite has yet to be fulfilled. What was apparent in both of the above-mentioned incidents was the powerful impact of the violence of one person upon the entire community. It is true that if left unattended, violence is contagious.

The community has shown itself to be a powerful influence in efforts to modify aggressive behaviour. In the same way, the community remains quite vulnerable to regression and subject to escalations in overall levels of aggression, should isolated aggressive incidents not be quickly and effectively addressed. Any manager of any type of milieu should be able to describe the contagiousness of violence, or the copycat behaviour that some types of destructive behaviours seem to precipitate. A study once done on *Sanctuary* statistically confirmed a "feeling" that incidents of self-mutilation and other acts of destruction of physical property seemed to occur in clusters. In the same way that actual physical aggression is, in itself, escalating in nature, so too can verbal aggression be a contaminant in an otherwise stable population. This is another reason why, in its definition of violent behaviour, *Sanctuary* has always had a most liberal and broadly defined concept of violence: as any behaviour, di-rect or indirect, that has a marked and destructive impact upon self or others. If this seems extraordinarily broad, so be it. By allowing for such a broad definition of violent behaviour, and by continually modelling intolerance to it, *Sanctuary*'s goal has been to use the therapeutic experience as an ongoing educa-tional workshop on violence rather than serving as a more medical-model treatment experience.

Despite constant monitoring, modelling, and mediating, there have been some occasions when violence, in its most ex-treme form, intruded upon the programme. The consequences of this intrusion have been devastating and remarkable. Twice in its 18-year history the unit has been the site of suicides by hanging. Twice, *Sanctuary* has served as a stage for an individual's choreographed ending, and each time there was, understandably, a profound impact upon patients and staff alike.

Suicide on the unit

After a staff member found a male patient hanging from a doorjamb in his room, *Sanctuary* was rocked by a convulsion of affect never experienced before by any clinician in the programme. Several patients had seen this victim of violence hanging, already dead, in his room. When senior management arrived within the hour (the event having occurred at around 10:00 p.m.), the unit more closely resembled a combat zone than it did a hospital. Patients were crying hysterically; many were mute. Some were screaming, some were still, and some were punching themselves or hitting their heads against the wall. Staff intervened as best they could, but this seemed to have only a minimal impact upon the initial frenzied response to this death. Eventually, a few of the more stable patients also began comforting the patients (including the previously discussed Norma B), and it was only after these patients began the process of helping to soothe those more severely impacted by this event that some semblance of order was restored.

The following day a community meeting was held to discuss the event and everyone's response to it. Uniformly, all spoke of the anger that was felt towards the person who violated *Sanctuary* by doing this deed, on the unit, during their hospital stay. Patients and staff alike spoke as people who had been subjected to violence, and no distinction was made by the role of the individual on the unit. This event had a powerful unifying and equalizing impact upon all who were a part of it. There was some discussion, of course, about the reasons why this individual had succumbed to such a violent end, and there was some appreciation of the pain and anger that must have prompted such behaviour. Without exception, however, patients and staff alike spoke of anger, and what occurred subsequent to this discussion and meeting was a powerful reminder of the potential for good that any powerful feeling can have, including feelings of anger, sadness, and fear.

Following the community meeting, all participants, staff and patients alike, split off into two groups, each group intent upon addressing issues of grief in its own way. The larger part of the community requested and pursued a ritual of purification of the unit, especially near the room where the death had occurred. The other, smaller part of the community, uncomfortable with such a ritual, was allowed to pursue its own, more private way of transiting from the trauma and shock experienced the night before. Without exception, not a single patient on the unit at that time exhibited any more self-destructive or self-mutilative behaviour. Not one person requested to leave the programme because it was "unsafe", and there were many who contributed their own personal gifts to the unit in the form of personal condolences to the programme. Songs, poetry, and a painting were all contributions from people who were not only impacted by violence, but who were struggling hard to find ways of transcending such violence.

The second suicide, which occurred approximately four years later, produced a similar reaction. The community initially wished to commemorate the deceased (a woman). Because of the beautifully landscaped location of the hospital, the suggestion was made to plant a tree in honour of the victim. There was considerable discussion about the wish to plant a living tree as a memorial to a person who had died by her own hand. The community decided to plant a tree in the grounds of the hospital and to dedicate it to all those who are survivors of abusive experiences. The intent was to use this traumatic event to inspire those still struggling with their own violent impulses, rather than commemorating one who used violence to end the struggle forever. There now stands, outside the *Sanctuary* at Friends Hospital, a weeping cherry tree dedicated to all those who have been injured by violence and who continue to fight against the forces and consequences of such violence.

Keeping a *Sanctuary* safe for nearly two decades has not been an easy task. It has required, minimally, a patient-to-staff ratio that is slightly higher than found in more traditional in-patient units. It has also required a constant monitoring and mainte-nance of community mores, as evidenced in the day-to-day programming, and this is where the availability and presence of on-site active management is critical for the maintenance of a safe milieu. As previously mentioned, violence is contagious. The availability of management to support line personnel is a critical element in the design of a safe milieu. This management must be well-versed in skills that do not emphasize shame as a deterrent to incorrect actions. All too often, management em-ploys a "shame-based" management style. This is a style of leadership in which the most important part of a problem-solv-ing strategy is the location of a person to blame, rather than the construction of a solution. The consequence of this type of man-agement is devastating. First and foremost, it discourages staff from using new and creative strategies in crisis management; strategies that emphasize control and quiet are used in prefer-ence to those that might be more therapeutically effective. Sec-ondly, staff in such an environment tend to become defensively entrenched, mostly in service of protecting their own jobs or reputations. Such a defensive posture can be extremely pro-vocative in times of crisis, for it tends to be dismissive of legiti-mate patient concerns about treatment issues. Such invalidation of real problems usually leads to an escalation of behaviours intended to draw attention. It is this escalation in the service of drawing attention, as much as any other factor, that leads to a situation where events start to spiral out of control. Violence is a course of action taken when other, less patently destructive ef-forts to secure need-gratification fail. Therefore, an environment that encourages individuals to become well versed and skilled in the art of listening is likely to be less prone to violent out-breaks.

Complementary to the ability to listen to an aggrieved in-dividual is the ability to speak to that person with the dignity and respect that all humans deserve. As police departments be-come more skilled in dealing with hostage situations and other situations in which violent outcomes seem imminent, they are trained in more effective strategies designed to maintain effective communication with the potentially dangerous person. As long as "negotiations" are taking place, it is possible to devise or stumble upon a non-violent solution to the problem. Too fast an effort to "fix" the problem before it is sufficiently understood often leads to increased alienation, resulting in an even greater likelihood that the outcome will be violent in nature.

When frustration replaces patience, staff efforts often escalate towards controlling the person and the situation, instead of reconciling differences. Although control is important to maintain, so too is the intent to address a problem. In the words of the immortal Janis Joplin, "freedom is just another word for nothing left to lose", and an individual who feels unheard, invalidated, and abandoned will also feel free to exercise a loss of control that can have a profound and long-lasting impact on self and others. When an aggrieved individual feels disenfranchised, powerless, blamed, and deprived of the legitimate use of his or her voice, a violent response is nearly inevitable. This type of response, as noted previously, may be either internally or externally directed, but it will invariably be destructive. In a trauma-based programme, the entire patient community consists of people who were deprived of safety and respect and of the effective use of their voices and, in most cases, of people who found themselves isolated to the point of being unheard, even if their voices did protest the abuse. Staff sensitivity to this point is crucial if violent re-enactments of past traumas are to be avoided.

Conclusion

This chapter reviews some very basic but vital constructs required in the never-ending struggle to harness the violence that is ready to be unleashed against self or others. There must exist a deep-seated and authentic belief that such behaviour is not an acceptable option to any but the most life-threatening of provocations, and then only to stop further violence. Similarly, there must be an authentic and energetic reminder that such behaviours are not acceptable in a programme dedicated to working with survivors of abuse or other traumatic events. These messages, coupled with an exceptionally broad-based definition of the meaning of violence, set the tone for any therapeutic discussion or intervention that follows. This belief must be incorporated as a non-negotiable norm, as inviolate as the neutrality of Switzerland has become. This standard of safe, protective authority models the kind of parenting experience that most *Sanctuary* residents have never previously experienced in the context of their own families of origin. In the absence of more constructive alternatives to conflict resolution and need gratification, violence becomes an acceptable recourse, and this is where the full and visible presence of all levels of management is required. Programs, hospitals, and communities that have uninterested, inaccessible, or disconnected administrations are not only deprived of the expertise and authority to create a climate conducive to change but, more importantly, may be less likely to have the full and enthusiastic support of line personnel and other ancillary staff to help teach and support non-violent community standards. Violence has always been an attractive short-cut to empowerment, and it is more likely to occur in a programme when there is an absence of active, caring, committed, and consistent management of the unit.

Even with active management of the unit, another critical element is required if there is to be an increased subscription to non-violent norms, and that is the active participation of each community member. Each person must feel empowered enough to believe that they do, in fact, play a significant role in keeping *Sanctuary* safe. This sense of importance and empowerment can be used in a few important ways. An expectation is explicitly set that if conditions in the community contribute to an increased sense of individual or collective vulnerability, people will feel emboldened and responsible enough to discuss the situation with other members of the patient and staff community. This can be especially difficult if such a discussion is interpreted as "telling on" another patient. In fact, this is one of the most common impediments to enlisting community support in monitoring community problems. Too often, it is believed that open discussions of a patient's difficulties or of the impact these difficulties might be having on the community constitute a form of betrayal of the patient. The message must be reinforced that such discussions actually empower the patient and the community. Failure to do so leads to increased secretiveness, anxiety, and a sense of impending doom. These feelings, more than any other, often serve as a reminder of earlier times, when abuse and danger appeared imminent. It is the failure to help in the monitoring process that ultimately leads to the degradation of a sense of safety and security.

Although much more could be said about responses to specific events that are precursors to violent or destructive outbreaks in a therapeutic milieu, it is more important to reaffirm one basic, most critical point. Those creating *Sanctuary* have noted, time and time again, that all people have an ability to raise themselves up to a higher, more constructive level of existence. Likewise, these people also have the ability to act out one's worst fears. What often accounts for the difference between a constructive sublimation of angry impulses and an explosive and dangerous response is the mind set and expectations of those staff who must engage with the survivors of trauma and abuse. Expect the worst and it is likely to happen. This is not to say that one must be ill-prepared to handle the worst. To the contrary, clinical preparedness is essential if the clinician is to maintain any credibility. But hopelessness can be read in the eyes of the clinician, and the survivor of a past trauma is extremely adept at perceiving whether the clinician does, indeed, have any hope for the individual. Time and time again, *Sanctuary* has worked with those who have failed in more traditional and restrictive in-patient programs. Reasons for a more successful outcome vary greatly, attributable, at least in part, to the inherent belief that all who participate in the *Sanctuary* programme not only are sufficiently empowered to improve the quality of their own personal lives, but can and should contribute to the improvement of the *Sanctuary* programme. This expectation is one of empowerment and hope and is often identified as one of the critical lessons learned or appreciated in the programme. An environment that promotes, teaches, encourages, and expects constructive resolution to long-standing problems is increasingly rare in today's health-care field. As economic factors dictate a more time-limited and less costly alternative to humane and respectful treatment, some very basic principles of recovery continue to be eroded. More frequently, there is an expectation that those who require treatment must be, by nature, so impaired and potentially dangerous that locked confinement and minimal therapy is acceptable. Not only is this position morally corrupt, but it is also, according to mental health regulations promulgated by many communities, patently illegal. People have a right to be treated in the least restrictive environment capable of meeting their therapeutic needs, and a presumption of a lack of control usually elicits the behaviours that are meant to be avoided.

As is apparent by now, keeping *Sanctuary* safe is a time-consuming, demanding, and, at times, difficult task. It requires a firm grounding in the principles of humane treatment and an equally firm commitment to principles of safety and the maintenance of boundaries. Most of all, it requires a belief that being subjected to violence is not, in itself, a condemnation to living a life of recreating similar violence. *Sanctuary* has been, and remains, a living workshop that attempts to demonstrate, on a daily basis, that the ongoing cycle of violence can, indeed, be broken. It is hoped that all who participate in *Sanctuary* eventually believe that it is their duty to ensure that the cycle of violence is broken.

CHAPTER FOUR

Conclusion:
a public health approach
to violence

Sandra L. Bloom

W hat is a public health approach to a problem as broad as human violence? Dr Adshead has given us a lyrical definition of the scope of violence and described how deeply embedded, how structurally important, violence is to human life and society. Dr de Zulueta has explored the violence that is endemic in our social institutions and has discussed the critical importance of attachment relationships in determining the causes and outcomes of violence. Mr Foderaro has provided us with some important lessons on how strictly and definitively violence must be contained if it is not to extend beyond its already extensive boundaries.

Taking all this into account, can we ever hope to establish what Immanuel Kant called a "perpetual peace"? This is an urgent question. Our understanding of the multigenerational effects of violence has been growing at the same time as the bloodiest century in the history of mankind has drawn to a close, dragging with it into this century a legacy of danger and threat. Global annihilation looms in the form of the detonation of nuclear devices, other nuclear disasters, chemical weapons, biological weapons, plague, and ecological disasters of many different sorts. If our growing understanding is to serve humankind, we will need to think and behave in a different way towards our fellows—all of them. At the end of the eighteenth century, Kant declared that "The peoples of the earth have thus entered in varying degrees into a universal community, and it has developed to the point where a violation of rights in one part of the world is felt everywhere" (Reiss, 1991, p. 108). If the global community we are presently developing is to survive without destroying itself, we must find ways to contain the bully in the school-yard so he does not become the bully in the boardroom or the war-room. We must attempt to minimize the damage that bullies have already done and to prevent more bullies from being raised, poisoned by the consuming energy of hatred required to annihilate the world.

A major obstacle to the pursuit of peace is the failure to comprehend that all of our human systems are "trauma-organized". Bentovim (1992) has explored this concept as applied to family systems in which abuse has occurred. He defines "trauma-organized systems" as "action systems", meaning,

> the essential actors in the system are the victimizer who "traumatizes" and the victim who is "traumatized". By definition there is an absence of a protector, or the potential protectors are neutralized. . . . The motto of those involved in the trauma-organized system is, First—"see no evil"; Second—"hear no evil"; Third—"speak no evil"; and the Fourth—"think no evil". It is not a question of the individual creating the system, or the system creating the problem. Events in the lives of individuals create "stories" by which they live their lives, make relationships, initiate actions, respond to actions, and maintain and develop them. Abusive traumatic events have an exceptionally powerful effect in creating self-perpetuating "stories" which in turn create "trauma-organized systems" where "abusive" events are re-enacted and re-inforced. [Bentovim, 1992, pp. xx–xxi]

The family unit is the first and most significant system that we encounter in our lives and, as such, remains the prototype for the development of all other systems. Thus far we have failed as a society to take into account the effects of unresolved transgenerational trauma on entire populations. We have not yet seriously considered how each of our systems other than the family—our school systems, criminal justice systems, financial systems, religious institutions, and value systems—may be profoundly influenced by the effects of unmetabolized and denied violence. Like individual victims of violence, without understanding the past and making different choices in the present, we simply assume that violence is unavoidable and normative, and we move into the future inevitably re-enacting a traumatic past.

Before Pasteur's discovery that invisible microbes were causing disease, we had to rely on "common sense" and historical experience to ward off disease. Sometimes these efforts worked, but more often they failed. Once we understood more about the causes of disease, we were able to develop a public health approach that helped eradicate diseases that had previously been untreatable, uncontainable, and unpreventable. This is precisely the point we have reached today in relation to the "disease" of violence. Like bacterial and viral disease, violence is contagious: it spreads through a population, is transmitted to the next generations, is insidious in its effects, and is often fatal (Bloom, 1995a).

A public health approach to violence means thinking broadly, synthetically, and collaboratively and most importantly, from the point of view of *prevention*. It means simultaneously focusing on the individual and the social context. Without such a focus, our treatment efforts can come dangerously close to enabling a destructively dysfunctional system. By providing society with the illusion that the effects of violence are treatable and curable, we may help provide justification for the status quo. We have a responsibility to make it clear that the fundamental reasons for our patients' suffering are not within the domains of personal vulnerability or genetic predisposition. Rather, the source of most human suffering is located within a socioeconomic and political context that supports and encourages violent perpetration (Bloom, 1995a, 1997; Bloom & Reichert, 1998; Herman, 1992).

Prevention activities attempt to accomplish three major goals: to deter predictable problems, to protect existing states of health, and to promote desired life objectives (Bloom, 1996). A public health approach focuses on prevention activities that occur at three levels: primary, secondary, and tertiary. Tertiary prevention aims at reducing the negative consequences of whatever disease has already occurred and is presently working its way through a population. Secondary prevention targets susceptible populations to alleviate conditions that are associated with acquiring the problem or disease. Primary prevention activities are directed at the general population with the goal of stopping the problem or disease before it starts. If we look at violence from the perspective of a public health problem, we can speculate about the changes that would need to occur in our society to curtail the spread of violence and to lay the groundwork for health (Bloom & Reichert, 1998).

Tertiary prevention

Tertiary prevention necessitates treating those who are already sick. But to enable our thinking to encompass the scope of the problem with violence, we must consider two levels of interventions—the individual and the social—simultaneously. As discussed in chapter three, the first critical step in recovering from the effects of violence is "safety". Therefore a focus question becomes: "What individual and social interventions are most likely to achieve safety?" and the next question becomes "What steps are we willing to take to achieve such safety?"

The first of these questions is far easier to answer than the second and is, to a great extent, a researchable, medical question. We know from our work with individual victims of violence that the continuation of violent perpetration in any of its forms must be strongly prohibited if healing is to occur (Bills & Bloom, 1998; Bloom, 1997; see also Foderaro, chapter three, this volume). From a medical perspective, this is fairly straightforward. After all, if a disease is being transmitted through contaminated water, the first thing to do is to stop people from drinking the contaminated water. If a disease is being transmitted by fleas, then public health efforts must be directed at finding a way to eradicate the infected fleas without doing further harm to the ecosystem.

Knowing what we now know about the way violence spreads through a family and through a community, a sane public health strategy requires the dedication of sufficient resources to ensure that those already victimized receive adequate treatment. With limited resources available, priority should be given to treating children and their caretakers. Violence intervention and treatment programs that support schools, day-care centres, domestic violence shelters, and refugee programs should be a high priority for any society. Combat veterans should be offered extensive services with particular focus on supporting improved parenting skills. Victims of crime are another at-risk population, and during the last 20 years extensive efforts have been made to provide better rights for crime victims.

Criminal justice efforts need to be directed at instituting firm measures that decrease the likelihood that violent offenders are allowed access to a never-ending supply of victims. This may indeed necessitate firm legal injunctions and imprisonment, to get chronic offenders off the streets and out of circulation. At the same time, offenders are an extremely high-risk population, and much more attention needs to be paid to treating and managing offenders more adequately so that we do not create more problems than we solve. Since our knowledge about the effects of violence is relatively new, the prison population has not had access to adequate treatment. As a result, we have no idea who is treatable and who is not. We do know, however, that prison environments are at present designed in ways that will increase, rather than decrease, further violence. We also know that the incidence of a past history of family violence, particularly child abuse, is extremely high in the criminal population, and these people remain largely untreated (J. Gilligan, 1996). Special efforts must be made in every community to spot the early signs of antisocial behaviour and to address it in its germinal form rather than waiting until the bullying, conduct-disordered child grows into a bullying, antisocial adult. These children and families need special attention from schools, law enforcement, the judiciary, social service agencies, physicians, and anyone in the community who can see trouble in the making.

Secondary prevention

In a public health approach, secondary prevention focuses on containing the infection that already exists and keeping it from spreading further. Priority is usually given here to utilizing interventions directed at those in the population who are at particularly high risk. Again, we must approach this subject from an individual and a social perspective simultaneously.

Containing violence means taking better care of families, particularly families already known to be at significant risk (Breakey & Pratt , 1991; Earle, 1995). This includes families that have already been victimized by violence, poor and single-parent families who lack adequate social support, and any families who suffer from unusual stress, such as dealing with disabilities, chronic illness, or members in prison. Special programmes need to be created to deal with children who have witnessed violence, particularly domestic violence, so that they do not automatically follow in the footsteps of their elders, and these programs must directly address issues of gender identity and violence. Widespread training must occur in all social settings so that providers in health and social service agencies are able to assess adequately and intervene in situations where violence has occurred. Health care providers are key because they provide a vital interface between the family and the broader community and are most likely to see the immediate aftermath of violent perpetration (Bloom & Reichert, 1998). Programmes designed to train general practitioners, emergency-room personnel, and other medical staff are critical to early intervention. In schools, troubled children sit right next to children who are doing well. Properly trained school personnel can be instrumental in setting up intervention programs that provide at-risk children with the kind of attention they need to prevent further damage (Bloom, 1995b; Crouch & Williams, 1995; Watson, 1995).

Violence also occurs in the workplace, and efforts must be made to effect change by creating a "violence-free company culture" (Barrier, 1995a). This requires setting a zero-tolerance policy for any kind of violence, whether it is non-verbal, verbal, sexual, or physical (Barrier, 1995b). This intolerance of violence must extend even to threats. As Matthiason, a lawyer and specialist in workplace violence, has commented: "a threat can do independent damage and have tremendous psychological consequences. . . . It is in fact, the growth of threatening words and behaviour that has turned workplace violence into a major national phenomenon" (Barrier, 1995b, p. 19). Some companies, like Liz Claiborne and Polaroid, have taken on the challenge by establishing domestic violence programs that have teeth. Polaroid even allows employees flexitime and short-term leave as well as extended leave without pay to seek protection and legal recourse against domestic violence (McMurray, 1995).

Preventing the spread of violence necessitates finding strategies to deal with violent offenders that are more effective than prisons. Penitentiaries do not work, and they never really have, if by "working" we mean releasing people into society who can become useful and productive citizens. However, it is clear that if a society is to be kept safe, then with those people who are so damaged that they have to be prevented from doing more harm incarcerating them may be all that we are able to accomplish. As Judge Dennis Challeen of Wisconsin has pointed out (1986), when viewed objectively, the present system of incarceration seems absurd when our goals for offenders are contrasted with the actual results of our punitive methods:

- We want them to have self worth . . . So we destroy their self-worth.

- We want them to be responsible . . . So we take away all responsibilities.

- We want them to be part of our community . . . So we isolate them from our community.

- We want them to be positive and constructive . . . So we degrade them and make them useless.

- We want them to be non-violent . . . So we put them where there is violence all around them.

- We want them to be kind and loving people . . . So we subject them to hatred and cruelty.

- We want them to quit being the tough guy . . . So we put them where the tough guy is respected.

- We want them to quit hanging around losers . . . So we put all the losers in the state under one roof.

- We want them to quit exploiting us . . . We put them where they exploit each other.

- We want them to take control of their own lives, own their own problems, and quit being a parasite . . . So we make them totally dependent on us. [quoted in Zehr, 1994a, p. 8]

Successful experiments with the use of the therapeutic community model have been carried out in prisons on both sides of the Atlantic, starting with Maxwell Jones's early efforts (1968). Harry Wilmer founded a therapeutic community in San Quentin in 1961 and wrote of the men he saw there: "They are dependent and prisonized. They wish not so much to be rehabilitated as to be deinstitutionalized. It is a complex task to help the prisoners free themselves for the dependent gratification of prison and crime and renounce the rewards and types of satisfaction inherent in the criminal life" (Wilmer, 1964). Turner described a successful therapeutic community for adult felons in the 1970s (Turner, 1972). Other positive results have been found in prison-based therapeutic communities aimed at treating substance abusers (Barr, 1986; Martin, Butzin, & Inciardi, 1995; Wexler, 1986, 1995; Worth, 1995).

All of these changes, although entirely possible, can occur only within the context of revitalized communities. In the physical body, disease occurs when there is a break in the skin, the barrier that protects our internal environment from the external world, or when there is a break in the immune system, our internal protective barrier. In the microcosmic world of the therapeutic community, violence breaks out when there is a rift, a hole, in the net of safety and protection that a healthy community weaves around its members. The same is true in the community-at-large. But rebuilding—and revaluing—communities means setting different priorities for distributing and spending our accumulated wealth, and this requires a radical shift from our present immersion in what has been called "malignant capitalism".

Such a shift could, conceivably, come about if we were to arrive at a more sound, ecologically based public policy on a global level. Any practice or theory, if taken too far, becomes destructive. There is certainly evidence that the mass exploitation of natural and human resources for the sake of short-term profit without adequate investment in and protection of the future is a suicidal practice. The ecological movement and social movements directed at the achievement of human rights provide the philosophical basis for such a shift towards violence prevention. The development of a social will that is simultaneously committed to child protection and protection of the earth's ecological balance would, by necessity, commit us to a less violent future. One hopeful sign of movement in this direction is the "Convention of the Rights of the Child" adopted unanimously by the General Assembly of the United Nations on 20 November 1989, paving the way for ratification by each separate nation and the establishment of monitoring committees. There was a steady movement in this direction throughout the twentieth century. Previous declarations on the rights of the child were adopted by the League of Nations in 1924 and by the United Nations in 1959. It was felt that there was a need for a comprehensive statement on children's rights that would be binding under international law. So far, as of March 1998, 186 countries have ratified the Convention, the end of a long process that began in the 1979 International Year of the Child (United Nations, 1996). Although the United States has thus far failed to ratify the Convention, it is the only developed country not to have done so. The United Kingdom signed the convention on 19 April 1990 and ratified it on 16 December 1991; it went into force on 15 January 1992.

Civilization progresses through conceptual changes in values long before those values become working reality. Guaranteeing the civil rights of children and letting those rights determine spending priorities and social policies is revolutionary and, like any peaceful revolution, will take many years yet to put into effect. Nonetheless, it is a beginning and a good segue into a discussion of primary prevention.

Primary prevention

Primary prevention, in this context, refers to the development of "social immunity". What steps can we take as individuals, as families, within each group, each social service system, each social organization or institution to increase the resistance of the social body to violent perpetration and increase the likelihood of peace? Discussing the primary prevention of violence requires an active imagination. It compels us to picture what a non-violent, technologically advanced society might look like. Short of Gene Roddenberry's *StarTrek*, we have few models, real or imaginary, to guide us, since we relegate most Utopian fantasies to the sidelines and seldom engage in a visionary discourse. This is a sign of the impoverishment of imaginative life as we enter the twenty-first century..

In a society engaged in the primary prevention of violence, family life would be very different from the way it is now. Children would be raised in communities, and raising children would become the shared responsibility of everyone in the community, as would taking care of the elderly, the infirm, and the disabled. Parenting would be widely shared, and it would be open, not private, preventing opportunities for abuse and providing children with numerous options for healthy attachments. Such shared parenting would also reduce the burden on those parents who produce healthy children but are less interested in raising them than in seeing to other community tasks (Bloom, 1993; Glantz & Pearce, 1989).

Disputes between family members and between other members of the community would be handled through tried-and-tested conflict resolution techniques that would involve and be supported by the entire community. For 2,500 years, Buddhist monks and nuns have been utilizing practices of reconciliation within a group context that are clear, firm, compassionate, sensitive, and produce results (Hanh, 1987). Models for a criminal justice system that focus on restoring the wholeness of a community that has been ruptured by violent perpetration already exist. When infractions occurred, the justice system would have moved from a system based on retribution to one founded on restoration and restitution. Such a system would be constructed so that the needs of the victim would be respected, a pathway of restitution and healing for the perpetrator would be available, and the need for the restoration of community harmony and wholeness would be paramount (Bianchi, 1995; Zehr, 1990). There would be no intent to punish people if such punishment could do more harm than good. The community would find ways to help those who offend against community rules to stop doing so and to start making positive contributions. We would learn to recognize bullies for what they are and not flatter them by calling them "strong", "powerful", "successful", or "masculine". Anyone who continued to harm others would be contained in whatever way was necessary to prevent violence, as long as the constraints were non-violent ones.

Education would be highly valued as a source of pleasure, entertainment, stimulation, and success in a community of peace. Schools would be contiguous with and relatively integrated with the rest of the working community. Children would be expected to learn emotional and relational skills alongside their academic pursuits. They would be taught how to work together in groups to resolve complex problems, rather than relying on the limited benefits of rivalry and competition. Classrooms would serve as rehearsal rooms for becoming healthy and contributing members of the adult community (Bloom, 1995b). The processes of continued growth, education, and the expansion of skills would continue into adulthood through the workplace, where creativity, interpersonal abilities, decision-making skills, and good judgement would be as valued as much as dedication to the job. The media would play a critical role in educating the public about everything they would need to know in order to create and sustain a safe and healthy living environment.

In a non-violent, technologically advanced society we would take much better care of our emotional, mental, and physical health. To do this we would learn to relax, to exercise, to laugh a lot, to have time off. We would learn to value relationships and creative expression over the possession of unnecessary material goods. We would learn to appreciate and celebrate diversity simply because it makes life so much more interesting. Over time, as an entire cultural system, we would learn to redistribute wealth, so that generosity would be more highly valued than personal self-aggrandizement. In an evolved, non-violent culture, engagement in the arts would be recognized as a vital, health-promoting activity for every human being, not a luxurious—and frequently dispensable—indulgence. Through this increased engagement with the arts, we would learn to express controversy and conflict through the non-violent exploration of complexity that can only be expressed through our innate creativity. The arts help us to touch our passion, our intuition, and our sense of wholeness with all of creation and provide us the means by which integration of contradictions and apparently irreconcilable conflict becomes possible.

Once we take the primary prevention of violence seriously, we will do all this, change in all these ways, not because we are transformed into angelic beings but because these changes are critical to our self-interest, to our survival. This was one of the arguments Kant gave for proposing a "perpetual peace": that it was in our fundamental self-interest to create such a peace as the world became a cosmopolitan community. We are seeing the evolution of this proposal. In every area of human pursuit, in each discipline, there is another view of a potential and more life-supporting reality emerging: in business (Estes, 1996; Maynard & Mehrtens, 1993; Ray & Rinzler, 1993), in politics (Lerner, 1996; McLaughlin & Davidson, 1994), in basic science (Bohm & Edwards, 1991; Darling, 1993; Davies, 1983; Margenau & Varghese, 1992), in education (Levine, Lowe, Peterson, & Tenorio, 1995), in criminal justice (Bianchi, 1995; Zehr, 1990), in religion (Blumenthal, 1993; Davis, 1994), a different paradigm, a different way of viewing nature and our role in it is struggling to be born.

In the end, it comes down to asking the question, "What steps are we willing to take to create a safe society?" This is a thorny one, and the answer differs enormously from society to society and even from one locale to the next. It inevitably leads to questions of political and social rights and responsibilities, regardless of the dangers to individual and social health. We know that weapons are a serious threat to public health and safety. And yet, depending on the country and the political climate, carrying a gun may be seen as an intrinsic and inalienable individual right. In the United Kingdom, the abolition of handguns was seen as a continuation of a long-standing and sane unwillingness to promote easy access to weapons of destruction. At the same time, in the United States possession of a handgun is seen as a basic and fundamental right, a primary defence against the abuse of power by the state, a symbol of freedom. For both countries, however, the production and distribution of weapons is perceived as an economic necessity. Similarly, a wealth of research may prove that pornography contributes to the creation of an environment promoting violence against women, but the restriction of pornography may impinge on our precious right to freedom of speech, or pornography may be seen as a perfectly harmless—or even helpful—male indulgence. Attempts to eliminate corporal punishment are met with fervent protests on the part of parents who believe that the state has no right to make decisions about their right to raise their own children, others who believe that physical punishment of children is commanded by God, and still others who do not have a clue how to raise children without hitting them. Creating laws to protect against media violence can infringe on the freedom of the press, and claims are often made that media violence is actually good for us—or, if not good, at least harmless. Our market economy supports and promotes measures that increase unemployment in segments of the population that are most vulnerable to the effects of poverty. Putting thousands of men and women out of work and plunging whole communities into poverty is seen as "good business" and completely and shamelessly justified. Affirmative action plans used to address racial and sexual discrimination are accused of producing reverse discrimination. We have had many examples, in the past century, of leaders using "safety" and "national security" as excuses for the most violent extremes of behaviour and deprivation of human rights. Still, there is something wrong with the discourse when license or repression are the only alternatives.

Years ago, one of our patients was deeply involved in what was a profoundly personal and political discussion of rights, and how the freedom of rights that her parents had enjoyed allowed the circumstances to exist that led to her abuse—a violation of her rights as a human being. She pointed out that in the United States, we benefit greatly from our Bill of Rights, but what is missing is a Bill of Responsibilities. What we have learned in the practice of maintaining a therapeutic community is that rights must always be balanced with responsibilities. In an interconnected community, even one as small as a family, should anyone have the *right* to inflict injury upon another person? And if injury is inflicted, what responsibility goes along with that right? If a parent beats a child and that child grows up to be an adult who uses violence against others—who is responsible? If a child is starved, beaten, and tortured in a society that permits and encourages such treatment, should the responsibility remain solely with that child as an adult, when that child commits a criminal act? As we gather increasing evidence that exposure to violence may permanently damage development, what responsibility does society as a whole have in preventing that damage from ever happening in the first place?

We have also learned that only non-violence can stop violence. Jesus, Gandhi, and Martin Luther King were all correct. Gandhi said, "I object to violence, because, when it appears to do good, the good is only temporary; the evil it does is permanent" (Wallis, 1994, p. 190). But non-violence does not mean silence. As Martin Luther King wrote in his letter from the Birmingham Jail, "I have earnestly opposed violent tension, but there is a type of tension which is necessary for growth . . . so must we see the need for non-violent gadflies to create the kind of tension in society that will help men rise from the dark

depths of prejudice and racism to the majestic heights of understanding and brotherhood" (King, 1990, p. 69). Non-violence
and social responsibility comprise the middle road, the alternative to freedom without responsibility and security without
freedom.

Barriers to change

Joseph Schwartz has pointed out that creative moments in science represent the conjunction of complex social events. Using
the cosmological debates of the seventeenth century, he has
shown how, during a major shift in historical consciousness,
science and the existing order can come into conflict (Schwartz,
1992). Judith Herman has pointed out that our recognition and
understanding of the effects of violence on human beings is
dependent on a social movement. Without such a movement,
the knowledge can be lost again, as it has been in the past
(Herman, 1992). History does repeat itself, and if we are not
careful, history will repeat itself once again, and the knowledge
that we have gained since World War II about the profound
effects of human trauma will be lost—or more likely, misinter-
preted—once again.

As long as science supports the established social order, the
pursuit of knowledge is safe. But history tells us that when
science begins to challenge our deeply entrenched beliefs and
institutions, science and those who pursue its values may be
punished. The knowledge we are gaining about the effects of
violence in all its forms attacks the deeply ingrained system of
structural violence that is the bedrock of our civilization. The
study of trauma and attachment challenges many fundamental
notions about the nature of human development and the nature
of human nature.

One of our social bedrock ideas is encompassed by the concept of *deviance*. Today, the criminal population and the mentally ill represent deviance. Regardless of the form of the
deviance, by definition the problem resides clearly within
the deviant person. Uncovering causality is not as important as

affixing culpability for the deviant acts. Providing explanations for deviant behaviour is usually derided as "making excuses for bad behaviour" and is therefore dismissed. Children are expected, at 16, 18, or 21, automatically to become responsible adults, and failure to do so is marked as deviant behaviour, punishable by society's rules. Trauma theory challenges our basic assumptions about deviance because it places the aetiology of most mental health and criminal problems in the space that connects the individual with his or her social group. If we come to believe that deviance is a result of injury sustained at the hands of another, much as a tree bent by a boulder grows in a deviant direction from its normal axis, then we move from an illness model to an injury model. An illness model places the responsibility for deviance directly in the lap of the deviant person. An injury model makes the deviance relational; other people are immediately involved as causative agents in the individual's distress and deviant behaviour. This is a particularly poignant reality in the case of abused and neglected children, who were powerless to stop the injury being perpetrated against them. Such a model confuses our otherwise clear-cut definitions of goodness and badness. In such cases, after all, who is more wrong, the criminal who commits the act or the society that failed to protect the criminal from harm as a child? When retribution is so basic to human nature, can we fail to understand the ways in which the criminal attempts to "get even" for such a basic betrayal by hurting others, and the mentally ill victim takes out the vengeance on him/herself?

The issue of retribution is another fundamental social structure, the bedrock of our criminal justice system. The desire for revenge comes easily and naturally to human beings, and control of the urge for vengeance comes as a result of maturity and moral development. Our understanding about how deeply violence can scar and skew the development of victims leads us to understand their desire for vengeance, even when that vengeance is sought through hurting others. So whom do we punish? And why do we punish? And when—if ever—does traumatic punishment do more good than harm? Jesus, Gandhi, Buddha, Martin Luther King, Nelson Mandela, Vaclav Havel are all leaders whom we hold in profound respect because they chose not to act on the urge for vengeance but, instead, provided us with an alternative, more loving, and more integrated approach. And yet, questioning retribution and punishment poses a serious threat to criminal justice systems whose laws, regulations, and practice are based on an established and accepted view of individual pathology and culpability alongside the right of the State to exact legal revenge.

Similarly, in the case of the mentally ill, it is convenient for the present social order to pretend that the cause of mental illness will be found in the genes and in fundamental, individual biological irregularities. If this is so, we are compelled to do nothing except wait for science to find a "cure". We do not have to address poverty, family violence, sexism, racism, the routine abuses of power in a family or in a country, because these problems can be kept safely separate from the biology of the mentally ill. At the same time, we discount the profound biophysiological consequences of exposure to violence and presume to believe that these consequences are not determining action and undermining our long-held belief in "free will".

The medical model is based on a fundamental split between mind and body, first clearly articulated by Descartes and deriving from the seventeenth-century conflict that necessitated a compromise solution to keep religious beliefs separate from science so that science could safely be pursued (Schwartz, 1992). The study of the effects of violence challenges this fundamental split. Our understanding of trauma has illustrated a number of critical interfaces between behaviour, development, and basic biochemical changes in the body and the brain. Those who remain firmly committed to the existing model can be profoundly disturbed by the suggestion that simple acts of changing the way we speak to other people, or of participating in theatre or painting or dancing or ritual, or the simple act of putting feelings into words in a safe social space can bring about profound physiological changes. The growing recognition that multiple personality disorder is actually fairly common and a useful defence in childhood against overwhelming exposure to violence challenges cherished notions of self, mind, and mental structure that provide a fundamental stability for the psychiatric professions that many are unwilling to give up.

Many centuries ago, when science split off mind/soul/spirit, it also dispensed with the need to study feelings. But now the study of emotions has crept back in, partially due to the growing recognition that most behaviour problems are a result of a failure to modulate emotions properly and that these modulation difficulties are a direct result of exposure—particularly chronic exposure—to violence. Finding an important role for feelings in our existing paradigm is awkward. Emotions, like intuitions, are traditionally feminine, irrational, a bothersome interference with rational thought. Allowing space for considering people's feelings, for compassion and sensitivity is ideologically threatening. Only children, women, homosexuals, and artists are supposed to be dominated by feelings, particularly the "gentler" emotions. The necessity of confronting the emotional nature of our basic biology and identity is threatening to a system grounded in the objectivity and unemotional nature of rationality.

Another deeply troubling structure that trauma theory challenges is our definition of what actually is "rational" and what is "irrational". By our present social definitions, anything that makes money is rational. Hoarding money and accumulating great unspent wealth is rational. Polluting the environment, selling weapons of mass destruction, depriving people of health care, allowing children to starve in poverty is "rational", as long as these are economically justifiable actions. Questioning the inherent sanity of our existing system verbally or non-verbally, directly or artistically, is "irrational" and potentially "immoral". Meanwhile notions of healing based on spiritual healing, mystical communion with a higher consciousness, even the need to "make meaning" are seen as fundamentally irrational and relatively unimportant. Suggestions that prayer, spiritual beliefs, alternative medicine, and psychic healing may affect immune systems and brain waves interposes the "irrational" in a very disconcerting way into the frame of that which is considered "rational".

Another troublesome social structure challenged by our understanding of the effects of violence is our attitude toward and treatment of children. Historically, children have been viewed as parental possessions, with few rights of their own. Anything a child said could be construed as a fantasy or a lie, since children were born with an evil and rebellious nature that had to be beaten into obedience and submission to authority (Ellison & Bartkowski, 1997). Our deep ambivalence about children has for centuries been cloaked in a syrupy sentimentality that has denied them their full humanity as well as their legal rights,. But we know now—not just in a literary but in a scientific sense—that the "child is father to the man". Early childhood development largely determines adult behaviour. This means that we must pay far more attention than we have done in the past to the well-being of children, and our present social structure does not fully support that kind of change.

Finally, the study of violence pushes us to redefine rights and responsibilities. It brings us right up against thousands of years of religious conceptualization on the relationship between human beings and a greater power. What is "free will" if, in fact, we do not really have control over our lives as long as we are tied to the unmetabolized events of a personal and transgenerational past? What is "original sin"—a concept still influencing our criminal justice system—when we begin to wrestle with the findings on multigenerational transmission of trauma? Is violence ever justified? Is it as wrong to fail to protect as it is actively to harm? What separates individual from social responsibility? Are we, in fact, "our brother's keeper"?

The social historian Fernand Braudel has said, "A civilisation generally refuses to accept a cultural innovation that calls in question one of its own structural elements. Such refusals or unspoken enmities are relatively rare: but they always point to the heart of a civilisation" (Braudel, 1994, p. 29). In this, the most violent of all centuries, we are forced to call into question many of our "deep structures" if we want to survive. Just as individual victims of violence must challenge the destructive experiences, beliefs, and values that for them have become normative, so we have a responsibility to challenge those experiences, beliefs, and values that continue to promote war, violence, and destruction. We must even challenge the fashionable, yet inherently cowardly, cynical notion that a "universal community" living in "perpetual peace" is an impossibility, a foolish utopian fantasy. The arrogance of cynicism is an excuse for laziness, a rationalization of self-destructiveness, and a failure of imagination. The Bible tells us that without vision, a people perish. If we are unable—or unwilling—to envisage a perpetual peace soon, in this case it could apply to *all* people.

REFERENCES

Adshead, G., & Morris, F. (1995). Another time, another place: the need for a forensic service for women. *Health Service Journal*, February 9: 24–26.

Agazarian, Y. (1994). The phases of group development and the systems centered group. In: V. Schermer, & M. Pines (Eds.), *Ring of Fire* (pp. 36–85). London: Routledge.

Ainsworth, M. D. S., Blehar, M. C., Waters, E., & Wall, S. (1978). *Patterns of Attachment: a Psychological Study of the Strange Situation*. Hillsdale, NJ: Erlbaum.

Amini, F., Lewis, T., Lannon, R., Louie, A., Gaumbacher, G., McGuiness, T., & Zirker Schiff, E. (1996). Affect, attachment, memory: contributions towards psychobiologic integration. *Psychiatry, 59*: 213–239.

Andreas, J. (1993). *Why the U.S. Can't Kick Militarism*. Philadelphia, PA: New Society Publishers.

Attanucci, J. (1988). In whose terms: a new perspective on self, role and relationship. In: C. Gilligan, J. V. Ward, & J. Taylor (Eds.), *Mapping the Moral Domain* (pp. 210–224). Cambridge, MA: Harvard University Press.

Bakowski, M., Murch, M., & Walker, V. (1983). *Marital Violence: The Community Response*. London: Tavistock Publications.

Barclay, G., Tavares, C., & Prout, A. (Eds.) (1995). *Information on the*

Criminal Justice System in England and Wales. London: Home Office Research and Statistics Department.

Baron, L., & Straus, M. A. (1988). Cultural and economic sources of homicide in the United States. *Sociological Quarterly, 29*: 371–390.

Barr, H. (1986). Outcome of drug abuse treatment in two modalities. In: G. DeLeon & J. T. Ziegenfuss (Eds.), *Therapeutic Communities for Addictions*. Springfield, IL: Charles C Thomas.

Barrier, M. (1995a). Creating a violence-free company culture. *Nation's Business, 83* (2): 22–23.

Barrier, M. (1995b). The enemy within. *Nation's Business, 83* (2): 18–24.

Bavidge, M. (1989). *Mad or Bad?* Bristol: Bristol Classical Press.

Belsky, J. (1980). Child maltreatment: an ecological integration. *American Psychologist, 35*: 320–335.

Bentovim, A. (1992). *Trauma-Organized Systems*. London: Karnac Books.

Bettelheim, B. (1960). *The Informed Heart*. London: Free Press.

Bianchi, H. (1995). *Justice as Sanctuary: Toward a New System of Crime Control*. Bloomington, IN: Indiana University Press.

Bills, L. J., & Bloom, S. L. (1998). From chaos to sanctuary: trauma-based treatment for women in state hospital systems. In: B. Labotsky Levin, A. K. Blanch, & A. Jennings (Eds.), *Women's Health Services: A Public Health Perspective*. Thousand Oaks, CA: Sage.

Bloom, M. (1996). *Primary Prevention Practices*. Thousand Oaks, CA: Sage.

Bloom, S. L. (1993). Psychodynamics of preventing child abuse. *Journal of Psychohistory, 21* (1): 53–67.

Bloom, S. L. (1995a). The germ theory of trauma: the impossibility of ethical neutrality. In: B. H. Stamm (Ed.), *Secondary Traumatic Stress: Self Care Issues for Clinicians, Researchers and Educators* (pp. 257–276). Lutherville, MD: Sidran Foundation.

Bloom, S. L. (1995b). Creating sanctuary in the classroom. *Journal for a Just and Caring Education, 1* (4): 403–433.

Bloom, S. L. (1997). Creating sanctuary: toward the evolution of sane societies. New York/London: Routledge.

Bloom, S. L. (1997). *Creating Sanctuary: Toward the Evolution of Sane Societies*. New York: Routledge.

Bloom, S. L., & Reichert, M. (1998). *Bearing Witness: Trauma and Social Responsibility*. Binghamton, NY: Haworth Press.

Blumenthal, D. R. (1993). *Facing the Abusing God: A Theology of Protest*. Louisville, KY: Westminster/John Knox Press.

Bohm, D., & Edwards, M. (1991). *Changing Consciousness: Exploring the Hidden Source of the Social, Political, and Environmental Crises Facing Our World*. San Francisco, CA: HarperSanFrancisco.

Bowlby, J. (1969). *Attachment and Loss, Vol. 1: Attachment* (2nd edition). London: Hogarth Press.

Bowlby, J. (1973). *Attachment and Loss, Vol. 2: Separation, Anxiety and Anger*. London: Hogarth Press.

Bowlby, J. (1980). *Attachment and Loss, Vol. 3: Loss, Sadness and Depression*. London: Hogarth Press.

Bowlby, J. (1984). Violence in the family as a disorder of attachment. *American Journal of Psychoanalysis, 44*: 9–27.

Bowlby, J. (1988). *A Secure Base: Clinical Applications of Attachment Theory*. London: Routledge.

Boyd, W. D. (Chairman) (1994). *A Preliminary Report on Homicide. Steering Committee of the Confidential Inquiry into Homicides and suicides by Mentally Ill People*. London: Royal College of Psychiatrists.

Braudel, F. (1994). *A History of Civilizations*. New York: Penguin.

Breakey, G., & Pratt, B. (1991). Healthy growth for Hawaii's "Healthy Start": toward a systematic statewide approach to the prevention of child abuse and neglect. *Bulletin of National Center for Clinical Infant Programs, 11*: 16–22.

Bremner, J. D., Randall, P., Scott, T. M., Bronen, R. A., Seibyl, J. B., Southwick, S. M., Delaney, R. C., McCarthy, G., Charney, D. S., & Innis, R. B. (1995). MRI-based measures of hippocampal volume in Vietnam combat veterans. *American Journal of Psychiatry, 152*: 973–981.

Brown, L. M., & Gilligan, C. (1992). *Meeting at the Crossroads: Women's Psychology and Girls' Development*. Cambridge, MA/London: Harvard University Press.

Brzezinski, Z. (1993). *Out of Control: Global Turmoil on the Eve of the 21st Century*. New York: Charles Scribner's.

Buchanan, A. (1996). *Cycles of Child Maltreatment: Facts, Fallacies and Interventions*. Chichester: John Wiley.

Challeen, D. A. (1986). *Making It Right: A Commonsense Approach to Criminal Justice*. Aberdeen, SD: Melius & Peterson.

Childhood Matters (1996). "Report of National Commission of Enquiry into the prevention of child abuse." Chaired by Lord W. Mostyn.

Chodorow, N. L. (1994). *Femininities, Masculinities and Beyond*. London: Free Association Books.

Christie, N. (1995). *The Crime Control as Industry: Towards Gulags, Western Style?* New York: Routledge.

Cooke, D. J. (1991). Violence in prisons: the influence of regime factors. *Howard League Journal, 30*: 95–109.

Cox, M. (1973). I took a life because I needed one: psychotherapeutic possibilities with the schizophrenic offender patient. *Psychotherapy & Psychosomatics, 37*: 96–105.

Cox, M. (1990). Psychopathology and the treatment of psychotic aggression. In: P. Bowden & R. Bluglass (Eds.), *Principles and Practice of Forensic Psychiatry* (pp. 631–640). Edinburgh: Churchill Livingstone.

Crouch, E., & Williams, D. (1995). What cities are doing to protect kids. *Educational Leadership, 52* (5): 60–63.

Darling, D. (1993). *Equations of Eternity*. New York: Hyperion.

Davies, P. (1983). *God and the New Physics*. New York: Touchstone.

Davis, W. T. (1994). *Shattered Dreams: America's Search for Its Soul*. Valley Forge, PA: Trinity Press International.

Day Lewis, C. (1947). *The Poetic Image*. London: Jonathan Cape.

Delgado, J. M. R. (1968). Recent advances in neurophysiology. In: *The Present Status of Psychotropic Drugs*. Excerpta Medica International Congress Series 180 (pp. 36–48). New York: Excerpta Medica.

Dell, S., Robertson, G., James, K., & Grounds, A. (1993). Remands and psychiatric assessments in Holloway prison. *British Journal of Psychiatry, 163*: 634–644.

Dobash, R. E., & Dobash, R. P. (1980). *Violence against Wives: A Case Against*. London: Open Books/Sage.

Dyer, C. (1990). Conjugal wrongs. *Guardian*, 28 November.

Earle, R. B. (1995). *Helping to Prevent Child Abuse—and Future Criminal Consequences: Hawai's Healthy Start*. Washington, DC: U.S. Department of Justice, National Institute of Justice.

Ellis, D. (1992). The deadliest year yet. *Time*, January, p. 25.

Ellison, C. G., & Bartkowski, J. P. (1997). Religion and the legitimation of violence. In: J. Turpin & L. R. Kurtz (Eds.), *The Web of Violence: From Interpersonal to Global* (pp. 46–67). Urbana, IL: University of Illinois Press.

Estes, R. (1996). *Tyranny of the Bottom Line: Why Corporations Make Good People Do Bad Things*. San Francisco, CA: Berrett-Koehler.

Estroff, S., Zimmer, C., Lachicotte, W. S., & Benoit, J. (1994). The influence of social networks and social support on violence by persons with serious mental illness. *Hospital and Community Psychiatry, 45:* 669–678.

Everywoman (1988). *Pornography and Sexual Violence: Evidence of the Links.* London: Everywoman

Farrell, W. (1993). *The Myth of Male Power.* New York: Simon & Schuster.

Finkelhor, D. (1983). Common features of family abuse. In: D. Finkelhor, R. J. Gelles, G. T. Hotaling, & M. Straus (Eds.), *The Dark Side of Families.* London: Sage.

Fonagy, P., Steele, M., Steele, H., Leigh, T., Kennedy R., Mattoon, G., & Target, M. (1995). Attachment; the reflective self, and border-line states: the predictive specificity of the adult attachment interview and pathological emotional development. In: S. Goldberg, R. Muir, & J. Kerr (Eds.), *Attachment Theory, Social, Developmental, and Clinical Perspectives.* Hillsdale, NJ/London: Analytic Press.

Fonagy, P., Target, M., Steele, M., Steele, L. T., Levinson, A., & Kennedy, R. (1997). Morality, disruptive behaviour; borderline personality disorder; crime and their relationship to attachment. In: L. Atkinson & K. Zucker (Eds.), *Attachment and Psychopathology* (pp. 223–276). London: Guilford Press.

Fraiberg, S., Adelson, E., & Shapiro, V. (1980). Ghosts in the nursery: a psychoanalytic approach to the problems of impaired infant–mother relationships. In: F. Fraiberg (Ed.), *Clinical Studies in Infant Mental Health: The First Year of Life.* London: Tavistock.

Gelles, R. J. (1978). Violence toward children in the United States. *American Journal of Orthopsychiatry, 48:* 580–592.

George, C., Kaplan, N., & Main, M. (1985). *The Adult Attachment Interview.* Privileged communication. Department of Psychology, University of California at Berkeley. [Also in: M. Main & R. Goldwyn (Eds.), *Assessing Attachment through Discourse, Drawings and Reunion Situations,* ed. New York: Cambridge University Press, in press.]

Gilligan, C. (1982). *A Different Voice.* Cambridge, MA/London: Harvard University Press.

Gilligan, J. (1996). *Violence: Our Deadly Epidemic and Its Causes.* New York: Grosset/Putnam.

Gilligan, J. (1997). *Violence: Reflections on a National Epidemic.* New York: Vintage Books.

Glantz, K., & Pearce, J. K. (1989). *Exiles from Eden*. New York: W.W. Norton.

Grevin, P. (1990). *Spare the Child: The Religious Roots of Punishment and the Psychological Impact of Physical Abuse*. New York: Vintage.

Guillamont, A., Puech, H., Quispel, G., Till, W., & Abd al Masih, Y. (1959). *The Gospel According to St Thomas*. London: Collins.

Gunn, J. (1991). Human violence: a biological perspective. *Criminal Behaviour and Mental Health*, 1: 35–54.

Hagan, J. (1994). *Crime and Disrepute*. London: Pine Forge Press.

Halperin, D. S., Bouvier, P., Jaffe, P. D., Mounoud, R.-L., Pawlak, C. H., Laederach, J., Wicky, H. R., & Astie, F. (1996). Prevalence of child sexual abuse among adolescents in Geneva: Results of a cross-section survey. *British Medical Journal*, 312: 1326–1329.

Hanh, Thich Nhat (1987). *Being Peace*. Berkeley, CA: Parallax Press.

Harlow, H. F. (1974). *Learning to Love* (second edition). New York/London: Jason Aronson.

Harlow, H. F., & Mears, C. (1979). *Primate Perspectives*. New York/London: John Wiley.

Herman, J. L. (1986). Histories of violence in an out-patient population: an exploratory study. *American Journal of Orthopsychiatry*, 56: 137–141.

Herman, J. L. (1992). *Trauma and Recovery*. New York: Basic Books.

Hobsbawm, E. (1994). *An Age of Extremes: The Short Twentieth Century*. London: Abacus.

Hobsbawm, E. (1997). Barbarism: a user's guide. In: E. Hobsbawm, *On History*. London: Weidenfield & Nicolson.

Hofer, M. A. (1984). Relationships as regulators, a psychobiological perspective on bereavement. *Psychosomatic Medicine*, 46: 183–197.

Holmes, J. (1996). *Attachment, Intimacy and Autonomy: Using Attachment Theory in Adult Psychotherapy*. Northvale NJ: Jason Aronson.

Janoff-Bulman, R. & Frieze, H. (1983). A theoretical perspective for understanding reactions to victimisation. *Journal of Social Issues*, 39: 1–17.

Jones, M. (1968). *Social Psychiatry in Practice*. Harmondsworth, Middlesex: Penguin.

Kagan, J. (1994). *Galen's Prophecy*. London: Free Association Books.

Kagan, J. (1997). Temperament and the reactions to unfamiliarity. *Child Development*, 68: 139–143.

Kaminer, W. (1995). *It's All the Rage: Crime and Culture*. New York: Addison Wesley.

Kennedy, H. G., & Grubin, D. (1992). Patterns of denial in sex offenders. *Psychological Medicine, 22*: 191–196.

King, M. L. (1990). Letter from the Birmingham Jail. In: R. L. Holmes, *Non-Violence in Theory and Practice* (pp. 68–77). Belmont, CA: Wadsworth Publishing.

Knight, R., & Prentky, R. (1990). Classifying sexual offenders and corroboration of taxonomic models. In: W. D. Marshall, D. Laws, & H. Babaree (Eds.), *A Handbook of Sexual Assault* (pp. 23–49). New York: Plenum.

Kohler, G., & Alcock, N. (1976). An empirical table of structural violence. *Journal of Peace Research, 13*: 343–356.

Korkenderfer, B., & Ladd, G. W. (1997). Victimised children's responses to peers' aggression: behaviours associated with reduced versus continued victimisation. *Development and Psychopathology, 9*: 59–73.

Kraemer, G. W. (1985). Effects of differences in early social experience on primate neurobiological–behavioural development. In: M. Reite & T. Field (Eds.), *The Psychobiology of Attachment and Separation* (pp. 135–161). London: Academic Press.

Lamb, M. (1997). Fathers and child development: an introductory overview and guide. In: M. Lamb (Ed.), *The Role of the Father in Child Development* (pp. 1–18). Chichester: John Wiley.

Lamb, S. (1990). Acts without agents: an analysis of linguistic avoidance in journal articles on men who batter women. *American Journal of Orthopsychiatry, 61*: 250–257.

Lees, S. (1997). *Ruling Passions, Sexual Violence, Reputations and the Law*. Buckinghamshire: Open University Press.

Lerner, M. (1996). *The Politics of Meaning: Restoring Hope and Possibility in an Age of Cynicism*. Reading, MA: Addison-Wesley.

Levi, P. (1989). *The Drowned and the Saved*. London: Abacus.

Levine, D., Lowe, R., Peterson, B., & Tenorio, R. (Eds.) (1995). *Rethinking Schools: An Agenda for Change*. New York: New Press.

Levinson, D. (1989). *Family Violence in Cross Cultural Perspective*. Thousand Oaks, CA: Sage.

Lewis, C. S. (1963). *A Grief Observed*. London: Faber & Faber.

Lifton, R. J. (1986). *The Nazi Doctors: Medical Killing and the Psychology of Genocide*. London: W. H. Allen.

Lifton, R. J., & Markusen, E. (1990). *The Genocidal Mentality: Nazi Holocaust and Nuclear Threat*. London: Macmillan.

Lindemann, E. (1944). Symptomatology and management of acute grief. *American Journal of Psychiatry, 101*: 141–149.

Link, B., & Stueve, A. (1994). Psychotic symptoms and the violent/ illegal behaviour of mental patients compared to community controls. In: J. Monahan & H. Steadman (Eds.), *Violence and Mental Disorder: Developments in Risk Assessment*. Chicago, IL: University of Chicago Press.

Lunde, D., & Sigal, H. (1990). Multiple victim killers. In: P. Bowden & R. Bluglass (Eds.), *Principles and Practice of Forensic Psychiatry* (pp. 625–630). Edinburgh: Churchill Livingstone.

Luntz, B. K., & Widom, C. S. (1994). Anti-social personality disorder in abused and neglected children grown up. *American Journal of Psychiatry, 151*: 670–674.

Main, M. (1981). Avoidance in the service of attachment, a working paper. In: K. Immelman, G. Barlow, M. Main, & L. Petrinovitch (Eds.), *Behavioural Development: The Bielefeld Interdisciplinary Project*. New York: Cambridge University Press.

Main, M., & Hesse, E. (1990). Parent's unresolved traumatic experiences are related to infant disorganised attachment staus: is frightened and/or frightening parental behaviour the linking mechanism? In: M. T. Greenberg, D. Cicchetti, & E. M. Cummings (Eds.), *Attachment in the Preschool Years* (pp. 161–182). Chicago, IL: Chicago University Press.

Malamuth, H. M. (1981). Rape proclivity among males. *Journal of Social Issues, 37* (4): 138–157.

Margenau, H., & Varghese, R. A. (1992). *Cosmos, Bios, Theos: Scientists Reflect on Science, God, and the Origins of the Universe, Life, and Homo sapiens*. LaSalle, IL: Open Court Press.

Martin, S. S., Butzin, C. A., & Inciardi, J. A. (1995). Assessment of a multistage therapeutic community for drug-involved offenders. *Journal of Psychoactive Drugs, 27* (1): 109–116.

Masters, B. (1986). *Killing for Company*. London: Coronet Books.

Maynard, H. B., & Mehrtens, S. E. (1993). *The Fourth Wave: Business in the 21st Century*. San Francisco, CA: Berrett-Koehler.

McCarney, W. (1996). Domestic violence. *British Juvenile and Family Courts Society Newsletter*, April, pp. 1–3.

McLaughlin, C., & Davidson, G. (1994). *Spiritual Politics: Changing the World from the Inside Out*. New York: Ballantine Books.

McMurray, K. (1995). Workplace violence: can it be prevented? *Trial, 31* (12): 10–13.

Meadow, R. (1989). Epidemiology of child abuse. *British Medical Journal, 298*: 727–730.

Milgram, S. (1974). *Obedience and Authority: An Experimental View*. London: Harper & Row.

Miller, J. (1996). *Search and Destroy: African–American Males in the Criminal Justice System*. New York: Cambridge University Press.

Monahan, J. (1997). Clinical and actuarial predictions of violence. In: D. Faigman, D. Kaye, M. Saks, & J. Sanders (Eds.), *Modern Scientific Evidence: The Law and Science of Expert Testimony, Vol. 1* (p. 309). St Paul, MN: West Publishing.

Monahan, J., & Steadman, H. (Eds.) (1994). *Violence and Mental Disorder: Developments in Risk Assessment*. Chicago, IL: Chicago University Press.

National Victim Centre (1993). *Crime and Victimization in America: Statistical Overview*. Arlington, VA: National Victim Centre.

Panksepp, J. (1984). The psychobiology of prosocial behaviour: separation distress, play and altruism. In: C. Zahn-Waxler, E. M. Cummins, & R. Ianotti (Eds.), *Social and Biological Origins of Altruism and Aggression* (pp. 16–57). Cambridge: Cambridge University Press.

Panksepp, J., Siviy, S. M., & Normansell, I. A. (1985). Brain opioids and social emotions. In: M. Reite & T. Field (Eds.), *The Psychobiology of Attachment and Separation* (pp. 3–49). London: Academic Press.

Patrick, M., Hobson, R. P., Castle, P., Howard, R., & Maughan, B. (1994). Personality disorder and the early representations of early social experience. *Developmental Psychopathology*, 94: 375–388.

Perry, B. D. (1994). Neurobiological sequelae of childhood trauma: PTSD in children. In: M. M. Murburg (Ed.), *Catecholamine Function in Posttraumatic Stress Disorders: Emerging Concepts*. Washington, DC: American Psychiatric Press.

Perry, B. D., & Pate, J. E. (1994). Neurodevelopment and the psychobiological roots of post-traumatic stress disorder. In: L. F. Koziol and C. E. Stout (Eds.), *The Neuropsychology of Mental Disorders: A Practical Guide*. Springfield, IL: Charles C Thomas.

Putnam, F. W. (1990). Disturbances of the "self" in victims of childhood sexual abuse. In: R. P. Kluft (Ed.), *Incest-Related Syndromes of Adult Psychopathology* (pp. 113–132). Washington, DC: American Psychiatric Press.

Rauch, S. L., van der Kolk, B. A., Fisler, R. E., Alpert, N. M., Orr, S. P., Savage, C. R., Fischman, A. J., Jenike, M. A., & Pitman, R. K. (1996). A symptom provocation study of posttraumatic stress disorder using positron emission tomography and script driven imagery. *Archives of General Psychiatry, 53*: 380–387.

Ray, M., & Rinzler, A. (1993). *The New Paradigm in Business: Emerging Strategies for Leadership and Organizational Change.* New York: G.P. Putnam's Sons.

Reiss, H. (1991). *Kant: Political Writings.* Cambridge: Cambridge University Press.

Robins, L. (1986). The consequences of conduct disorder in girls. In: D. Olweus, J. Block, & M. Radke Yarrow (Eds.), *Development of Antisocial and Prosocial Behavior* (pp. 385–414). London: Academic Press.

Rosen, I. (1989). Perversion as a regulator of self-esteem. In: I. Rosen (Ed.), *Sexual Deviation* (pp. 65–78). Oxford: Oxford University Press.

Russell, D. (1993). *Philadelphia Daily News* (3), 5 October.

Sabini, J., & Silver, M. (1982). *Moralities of Daily Life.* Oxford: Oxford University Press.

Salter, A. (1988). *Transforming Trauma.* Thousand Oaks, CA: Sage.

Sanday, P. R. (1981). The socio-cultural context of rape. *Journal of Social Issues, 37*: 5–27.

Schwartz, J. (1992). *The Creative Moment: How Science Made Itself Alien to Modern Culture.* London: Jonathan Cape.

Sereny, G. (1974). *Into That Darkness.* London: Andre Deutsch.

Sereny, G. (1994). *Albert Speer: His Battle with Truth.* London: Macmillan.

Showalter, E. (1987). *The Female Malady: Women, Madness and English Culture 1830–1980.* London: Virago.

Silver, S. M. (1986). An inpatient program for post-traumatic stress disorder: Context as treatment. In: C. R. Figley (Ed.), *Trauma and Its Wake, Vol. 2: Post-Traumatic Stress Disorder: Theory, Research and Treatment.* New York: Brunner/Mazel.

Smith, J. (1989). *Misogynies.* London: Faber & Faber.

Solomon, Z., Kotler, M., & Mikulencer, M. (1988). Combat related post-traumatic stress disorder among second generation Holocaust survivors: preliminary findings. *American Journal of Psychiatry, 145*: 865–868.

Sroufe, L. A., & Waters, E. (1977). Heart rate as a convergent measure in clinical and developmental research. *Merrill-Palmer Quarterly, 23*: 3–27.

Stern, D. (1985). *The Interpersonal World of the Infant: A View from Psychoanalysis and Developmental Psychology.* New York: Basic Books.

Sternberg, K. J. (1997). Fathers, the missing parents in research on family violence. In: M. Lamb (Ed.), *The Role of the Father in Child Development* (pp. 284–308). Chichester: John Wiley.

Stoller, R. J. (1975). *Perversion, the Erotic Form of Hatred.* New York: Pantheon [reprinted London: Karnac Books, 1989].

Storr, A. (1968). *Human Aggression.* Harmondsworth, Middlesex: Penguin.

Straus, M. B. (1991). Discipline and deviance: physical punishment of children and violence and other crime in adulthood. *Social Problems, 38*: 133–154.

Suomi, S. J. (1997). Early determinants of behaviour: evidence from primate studies. *British Medical Bulletin, 53*: 170–184.

Teicher, M. H., Glod, C. A., Surrey, J., & Swett, C. (1993). Early childhood abuse and limbic system ratings in adult psychiatric outpatients. *Journal of Neuropsychiatry and Clinical Neurosciences, 5* (3): 301–306.

Troy, M., & Sroufe, L. A. (1987). Victimization among preschoolers: role of attachment relationship history. *Journal of American Academy of Child and Adolescent Psychiatry, 26*: 166–172.

Turner, M. (1972). Norman House. In: S. Whiteley, D. Briggs, & M. Turner (Eds.), *Dealing with Deviants.* London: Hogarth Press.

United Nations (1996). *The Rights of the Child.* Human Rights Fact Sheet No. 10 (Rev. 1). New York: United Nations.

Van der Kolk, B. A. (1989). The compulsion to repeat the trauma: re-enactment, revictimization and masochism. In: *Psychiatric Clinics of North America, 12*: 389–411.

Van der Kolk, B. A. (1994). The body keeps the score: memory and the evolving psychobiology of posttraumatic stress. *Harvard Review of Psychiatry, 1*: 253–265.

Van IJzendoorn, M., Feldbrugge, J., Derks, F., de Ruiter, C., Verhagen, M., Philipse, M., van der Staake, C., & Riksen-Walraven, J. (1997). Attachment representations of personality disordered criminal offenders. *American Journal of Orthopsychiatry, 67*: 449–459.

Van IJzendoorn, M. H., & Bakermans-Kranenburg, M. J. (1997). Intergenerational transmission of attachment: a move to the contextual level. In: L. Atkinson & K. J. Zucker (Eds.), *Attachment and Psychopathology.* New York/London: Guildford Press.

Wallis, J. (1994). *The Soul of Politics.* New York: New Press.

Watson, R. (1995). A guide to violence prevention. *Educational Leadership, 52* (5): 57–60.

Watt, G. C. M. (1996). All together now: why social deprivation matters to everyone. *British Medical Journal, 312*: 1026–1029.

Weiler, B. L., & Widom, C. S. (1996). Psychopathy and violent behaviour in abused and neglected young adults. *Criminal Behaviour and Mental Health, 6*: 263–281.

Welldon, E. V. (1988). *Mother, Madonna, Whore.* London: Free Association Books.

Wexler, H. K. (1986). Therapeutic communities within prisons. In: G. DeLeon & J. T. Ziegenfuss (Eds.), *Therapeutic Communities for Addictions.* Springfield, IL: Charles C Thomas.

Wexler, H. K. (1995). The success of therapeutic communities for substance abusers in American prisons. *Journal of Psychoactive Drugs, 27* (1): 57–66.

Widom, C. (1989). Does violence beget violence? A critical examination of the literature. *Psychological Bulletin, 106*: 3–28.

Widom, C., & Ames, M. (1994). Criminal consequences of childhood sexual victimisation. *Child Abuse and Neglect, 18*: 303–318.

Wilmer, H. (1964). A living group experiment at San Quentin prison. *Corrective Psychiatry and Journal of Social Therapy, 10:* 6–15.

Wilson, C., & Seaman, D. (1990). *Serial Killers: A Study of the Psychology of Violence.* London: W. H. Allen.

Worth, R. (1995). A model prison. *Atlantic Monthly*, November, p. 38.

Wrangham, R., & Peterson, D. (1996). *Demonic Males: Apes and the Origins of Human Violence.* London: Bloomsbury.

Wilczynski, A. (1997). Mad or bad? Child killers, gender and the Courts. *British Journal of Criminology, 37*: 419–436.

Yehuda, R., & McFarlane, A. C. (1995). Conflict between current knowledge of Posttraumatic stress disorder and it original conceptual base. *American Journal of Psychiatry, 152*: 1705–1713.

Zehr, H. (1990). *Changing Lenses: A New Focus for Crime and Justice.* Scottsdale, PA: Herald Press.

Zulueta, F. de (1993). *From Pain to Violence. The Traumatic Roots of Destructiveness.* London: Whurr.

INDEX